WILDLIFE CONSERVATION DECODED

HOW ANYONE CAN UNLOCK THE SECRETS OF
WILDLIFE MANAGEMENT AND BIODIVERSITY, EVEN
WITHOUT A SCIENCE BACKGROUND

GOLDENPEDAL PUBLISHING

TABLE OF CONTENTS

INTRODUCTION

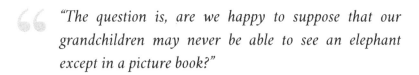 *"The question is, are we happy to suppose that our grandchildren may never be able to see an elephant except in a picture book?"*

— *DAVID ATTENBOROUGH*

David Attenborough's poignant question forces us to confront a grim reality: the looming extinction of Earth's magnificent creatures. It implores us to acknowledge humans' pivotal function in shaping our world's future. Our actions today will determine whether future generations bask in nature's wonders firsthand or merely glimpse them through the pages of history books. Conservation emerges as the imperative to secure our planet's legacy.

THE STARK MAMMAL POPULATION DIVIDE

In 2018, a study painted a startling picture of the global mammal population. The numbers speak volumes: wild animals constitute a mere 4 percent, humans dominate at 36 percent, and farm animals comprise 60 percent (Bar-On et al., 2018). These statistics unmask a disheartening reality—our planet's native inhabitants are dwindling at an alarming rate. The urgency of conservation efforts couldn't be more apparent; they are our last defense against ecological collapse. Each species holds value, and the time has come to safeguard our world's precious wildlife heritage.

These statistics underscore the monumental challenges surrounding wildlife conservation. We encounter formidable obstacles as we delve deeper into this topic, but the imperative to protect our planet's natural heritage has never been more crucial.

CHALLENGES YOU FACE IN WILDLIFE CONSERVATION

You carry a profound sense of responsibility and concern about the impact of human activities on wildlife. This concern has ignited a sincere desire to initiate positive change. You are not alone in feeling this way; countless individuals share your passion for nature and grapple with the looming shadow of climate change.

Your lifelong fascination with the natural world has intensified in light of recent climate developments. This concern has sometimes left you feeling overwhelmed as you strive to expand your understanding of wildlife conservation and its intricate connection to the pressing issue of climate change.

Your immediate objective is to boost understanding about wildlife conservation and disseminate knowledge to those eager to learn more. You recognize the power of sharing compelling facts and statistics to cultivate more understanding of our planet's current challenges and inspire others to take action.

Furthermore, you're contemplating a career in wildlife conservation, though you might need clarification about the motives driving this choice and the essential knowledge and skills required for a practical pursuit. There is a mix of daunting and exhilarating feelings as you contemplate dedicating your life to safeguarding wildlife and the environment.

Additionally, you've noticed the frequent use of specific terms and jargon in news and social media discussions regarding wildlife conservation and ecological management. Your urge to achieve a more in-depth understanding of these terms stems from your commitment to staying well-informed about global events and their repercussions on the natural world. You aim to be an informed advocate for wildlife conservation.

In light of these challenges and aspirations, your dedication to making a meaningful impact on wildlife conservation is evident. Your pursuit of knowledge and willingness to share it are vital steps toward addressing the challenges faced by wildlife and the environment. By acknowledging these concerns and interests, you are better prepared to embark on your journey to promote wildlife conservation and ecological awareness.

WHAT AWAITS YOU AFTER READING THIS COMPREHENSIVE GUIDE

You will embark on a structured journey by engaging with this book. It begins with building a solid foundation for wildlife conservation and culminates in a forward-looking perspective. This unique four-part framework sets this guide apart from typical university textbooks or niche manuals prevalent in the market. Unlike resources that merely scratch the surface, this book ensures you grasp the theory and practice of wildlife conservation.

However, what truly distinguishes this guide is its practicality. It's not merely about obtaining knowledge; it's about translating that learning into motion. As you progress from understanding wildlife conservation to exploring the intricacies of biodiversity, probing into the nuances of wildlife management, and envisioning the road ahead, you'll gain actionable strategies. These aren't generic tips but are rooted in the latest research, making it a perfect blend of knowledge and action.

As a result, your future self won't be a passive observer. Armed with newfound confidence, you will champion the cause of wildlife conservation. You'll be adept at effectively raising awareness and standing as a beacon of informed action. By reading this book, you choose a pathway to make a substantial difference to the planet.

Before this comprehensive guide, exploring wildlife conservation may have felt like navigating a bewildering maze. Many resources leave newcomers feeling overwhelmed. Even scouring the internet yielded confusing and contradictory information, making it frustrating to grasp the significance of the cause while feeling utterly lost.

However, with this all-encompassing guide, the essential knowledge you seek is within your reach. No more going through inexhaustible sources or being led astray. This book consolidates everything you need, serving as your guiding light. This is undoubtedly the book for those who are genuinely committed to making a difference.

In the face of mounting challenges, you stand at the precipice of a meaningful journey into wildlife conservation. The urgency of protecting our planet's natural heritage is paramount. With this guide, you possess the tools to make a genuine impact to shape a future where our grandchildren can witness the majesty of elephants and other incredible creatures in the living, breathing world they inherit. Your journey begins now.

1

THE IMPORTANCE OF WILDLIFE CONSERVATION

"Here we are, arguably the most intelligent being that's ever walked planet Earth, with this extraordinary brain, yet, we're destroying the only home we have."

— JANE GOODALL

Drawing inspiration from Jane Goodall's heartbreaking observation about the paradox of human intelligence and our often careless treatment of our planet, it becomes abundantly clear that our wisdom must focus on preserving the fabric of life that sustains us.

LET'S START WITH THE BASICS: WHAT IS WILDLIFE CONSERVATION?

Let's explore the essentials of wildlife conservation. In this pivotal domain, our actions can make a meaningful difference, ensuring that the rich tapestry of Earth's biodiversity remains intact for generations to come.

What Is Wildlife Conservation?

Wildlife conservation primarily revolves around protecting both plant and animal species within their natural habitats. Its foundational premise is the preservation of the biodiversity of our planet, ensuring that ecosystems thrive, evolve, and sustain life for generations to come.

The Purpose of Wildlife Conservation

Wildlife conservation aims to guarantee the survival and flourishing of various species within their natural environments. This protection extends beyond individual species and encompasses the habitats they reside in, acknowledging the intricate relationships that exist within an ecosystem.

Why Is Wildlife Conservation Important?

Our world has been experiencing unprecedented growth in the human population, leading to an over-consumption of natural resources. This surge in consumption and the resulting urban and agricultural expansion endangers critical habitats such as forests, wetlands, and grasslands. Such encroachments don't merely threaten individual species but have the potential to disrupt entire ecosystems.

Evolution of Wildlife Conservation Ideas

Historically, wildlife conservation centered around safeguarding specific animals, primarily in zoos or reserves. Over time, conservationists recognized the limitations of this approach. The focus has gradually shifted from individual animals to safeguarding their broader habitats and the ecosystems they are part of. This transformation acknowledges the interconnectedness of life and the symbiotic connections within ecosystems.

The Role of Wildlife Conservation in Ecology

Conservation plays a crucial function in preserving ecological balance. Disruption of a single species can create a cascade of changes, affecting others in the ecosystem. For example, eradicating a predator can overpopulate its prey, which can overgraze or deplete resources, resulting in habitat degradation.

Economic Value of Wildlife Conservation

Beyond the intrinsic value of wildlife and the moral imperative to protect it, there's a tangible economic value to conservation:

1. **Obtaining Natural Products:** Wild species are sources of numerous products we rely on daily. For instance, the rubber industry owes its existence to extracting latex from wild rubber trees.
2. **Tourism Industry:** Protected areas, national parks, and wildlife reserves draw millions of tourists annually. The

earnings from ecotourism often fund further conservation efforts. For instance, Kenya's Maasai Mara National Reserve attracts tourists worldwide to witness the iconic wildebeest migration, significantly contributing to the nation's economy.

3. **Animal Trade:** While the illegal animal trade threatens many species, regulated business can be sustainable and economically beneficial. Breeding and selling certain species under controlled conditions can reduce the pressure on wild populations.

4. **Plants with Medicinal Value:** Many plants have therapeutic properties invaluable to the pharmaceutical industry. For instance, the rosy periwinkle plant, native to Madagascar, produces compounds used in drugs to treat Hodgkin's lymphoma and leukemia.

Wildlife conservation is an ethical endeavor and an economic and ecological necessity. The challenges of a burgeoning human population and the strain on natural resources make protecting ecosystems and their inhabitants even more imperative. We can ensure a world where humans and wildlife coexist and thrive through global cooperation, legislative frameworks, and grass-roots initiatives.

A DARK PAST AFFECTING OUR FUTURE: SPECIES EXTINCTION

Human actions, from deforestation to pollution, have cast a long shadow on our planet's biodiversity. As species disappear, we confront the loss of wildlife and a jeopardized future for all.

What Is Extinction?

Extinction occurs when a species, be it a plant, animal, or microorganism, no longer exists, meaning no living members live on Earth. This can result from various factors, including habitat destruction, predation, disease, climate change, or resource competition.

Extinct Species List: A Glimpse into the Lost World

Species	Description	Reason for Extinction	Year of Extinction
Dodo Bird	A Mauritius-native flightless bird, the dodo is often synonymous with extinction. It was easy prey because of its absence of fear towards people and its lack of natural predators.	Overhunting by sailors and the introduction of invasive species	1681
Stellar's Sea Cow	A large marine mammal discovered by European explorers in the Bering Sea.	Overhunting	1768
Labrador Duck	A North American bird, the duck's habits and habitats are still a mystery.	Unknown, but possibly overhunting or habitat change	1875
Rocky Mountain Locust	Once swarmed in vast numbers across the western U.S.	Habitat destruction due to farming	1902
Thylacine	Also known as the Tasmanian tiger, it was a carnivorous marsupial native to Australia.	Overhunting, disease, and habitat loss	1936
Deepwater Cisco Fish	A freshwater fish native to the Great Lakes of North America.	Overfishing and competition with introduced species	1950s
Hawaii Chaff Flower	A plant species native to Hawaii.	Habitat destruction and invasive species	Late 20th century
Golden Toad	Indigenous to the Costa Rican woodlands.	Disease, habitat loss, and climate change	1989
St Helena Olive Tree	Indigenous to the isle of St Helena in the South Atlantic.	Habitat destruction	2003

Why Extinction Rates Are Concerning

The current rate at which species become extinct is alarmingly higher than the natural background rate. With 15,000 species currently threatened, it's not just about losing individual species but the ripple effect it causes on ecosystems, potentially disrupting vital services.

History's Alarming Signals: Five Mass Extinctions

- **End of the Cretaceous: The Dinosaurs' Demise**

Around 66 million years ago, the world witnessed one of its most renowned extinction events: the end of the Cretaceous period. This extinction is best known for the relatively sudden disappearance of the mighty dinosaurs, those colossal creatures that had roamed and ruled the planet for millions of years. Although the exact cause remains debated, many scientists attribute their downfall to a catastrophic asteroid impact, resulting in significant climatic shifts and ecosystem collapses.

- **Late Triassic: The Ocean and Land in Turmoil**

Approximately 200 million years ago, during the closing chapters of the Triassic period, the Earth faced another significant extinction event. This calamity wiped out many marine species and several terrestrial vertebrates. Volcanic activities, leading to drastic climate changes and ocean acidification, are among the leading theories explaining this widespread loss.

- **End of the Permian: Earth's Darkest Hour**

The end of the Permian era, around 250 million years ago, marks the most extreme extinction in world history. An astonishing 90 percent of all species vanished during this time, earning it the grim title of The Great Dying. Prolonged volcanic eruptions, which led to lethal greenhouse gases flooding the atmosphere and causing extreme temperature fluctuations, were likely culprits of this catastrophic event.

- **Late Devonian: When Seas Silenced**

The Late Devonian extinction, roughly 375 million years ago, is characterized by significant losses among marine species. Coral reefs, once prosperous and teeming with life, suffered greatly. Factors such as the spread of land plants—leading to oxygen depletion in the waters and potential asteroid impacts—might have triggered this marine catastrophe.

- **Late Ordovician: The Icy Grip of Death**

The Late Ordovician extinction, occurring about 445 million years ago, saw a massive decline in marine species. The planet underwent dramatic changes as glaciation events gripped the Earth, leading to drastic climate changes. This rapid shift in global temperatures resulted in habitat destruction, particularly in marine environments, driving many species to extinction.

These historical extinction events serve as sobering reminders of the planet's fragile balance and the inherent vulnerabilities of life in the face of dramatic environmental changes.

Are We in a Sixth Mass Extinction?

Unfortunately, yes. The present death rate is up to 1,000 times the natural speed, and with vast anthropogenic influences like deforestation, pollution, overfishing, and climate change, many scientists agree that we are in the early phases of the sixth mass extinction.

Is It Possible to Reverse Extinction?

While it's impossible to bring back extinct species, ongoing efforts like habitat restoration, conservation, and genetic research are avenues for exploration to prevent future extinctions and possibly reintroduce species on the brink. Conservation is our best bet, and it starts with understanding and action.

In a world where every species plays a pivotal role in the ecosystem, ensuring their survival is synonymous with securing our own. From the tiniest microbe to the gigantic mammal, every extinction is a lost page in the Book of Life, a book we're still trying to read and understand.

METHODS OF WILDLIFE CONSERVATION

Conservation isn't a one-size-fits-all discipline. What works in one habitat may not be successful in another. Variables such as location, unique ecosystem characteristics, and specific threats dictate the ideal conservation strategy. Understanding and addressing these nuances is pivotal to practical wildlife preservation.

Preservation and Restoration of Habitats

Preserving natural environments is of paramount importance for the preservation of biodiversity. Whether it involves safe-guarding wetlands to support the migratory bird population or establishing protected regions like national parks—for example, the Galápagos Islands—these measures are essential to provide secure areas for species to rest, reproduce, and find shelter. Such initiatives are crucial for sustaining the variety of life forms and the fundamental health of the ecosystems they inhabit.

Sustainable Practices and Resource Management

Encouraging environmentally friendly practices benefits both the natural environment and local economies. Embracing methods like shade-grown coffee cultivation helps preserve bird habitats and supports farmers. On a larger scale, initiatives like recycling play a significant role: recycling paper, for instance, contributes to preventing deforestation and protecting forest-dwelling species. Also, effective management of species' populations, including regulating hunting seasons, is vital for long-term survival.

Research, Monitoring, and Data Use

Scientific research guides our conservation efforts. We can better identify high-priority areas and strategize conservation efforts by monitoring tigers' movements or collecting genetic materials for seed banks. This foundation of knowledge allows us to respond promptly to urgent threats and adapt our strategies as necessary.

Legal and Practical Protections

Both legal frameworks and practical, on-the-ground interventions provide layers of protection for species. The recovery of the American bald eagle serves as a testament to the effectiveness of protective legislation. At the same time, anti-poaching patrols in African national parks exemplify proactive measures to guard against immediate threats.

Rehabilitation, Breeding, and Release

Certain species benefit from direct human intervention. Examples include the reintroduction of the California condor following its near-extinction and the rehabilitation and release of injured sea turtles, which ensure the health and resilience of species populations. Captive breeding programs, like the one for the Arabian oryx, and translocation efforts, like moving rhinos to safer zones, are concrete steps toward bolstering and balancing wildlife populations.

Education, Awareness, and Community Engagement

Public education serves as a cornerstone for many conservation initiatives. Through workshops on the role of bees in ecosystems or community tree-planting events, we empower individuals to make environmentally conscious choices and participate in preserving their local ecosystems.

Control of Invasive Species and Ecosystem Balance

Maintaining a balanced ecosystem sometimes necessitates intervention. Controlling or eradicating non-native species, like removing invasive rats from islands, helps protect and restore native wildlife populations and overall ecosystem health.

Conservation is a multifaceted discipline, demanding strategies tailored to specific needs. By understanding and leveraging these methods, we can hope to ensure the survival of our planet's diverse inhabitants.

LOOKING AT THE HISTORY: HOW WILDLIFE CONSERVATION HAS DEVELOPED

Wildlife conservation has evolved significantly from early individual initiatives to global collaborative efforts. As threats to biodiversity grew, our approaches adapted, reflecting our advancing knowledge and the escalating urgency to protect the planet's precious inhabitants.

The Rise of Wildlife Conservation: A Century-Long Journey to Global Awareness

Historically, humans viewed the Earth's resources, including wildlife, as vast and inexhaustible. However, the last hundred years have seen a significant shift towards recognizing the importance of wildlife conservation, driven by several key factors:

1. **Industrialization:** The rapid industrial growth in the twentieth century led to widespread habitat destruction. Denuded forests and polluted water sources directly impacted wildlife populations. As the consequences became evident, the need for conservation gained attention.
2. **Species Extinctions:** The demise of iconic species, such as the passenger pigeon and the dodo, were alarming wake-up calls. These irreversible losses highlighted the vulnerability of wildlife to human activities.
3. **Scientific Understanding:** Advancements in ecology and biology provided an understanding of the

complicated connections between species and their habitats. As our wisdom evolved, so did our knowledge of the long-term implications of biodiversity loss.

4. **Global Collaboration:** International treaties and conventions, like the Convention on Biological Diversity, brought nations together, signaling a unified commitment to protect global biodiversity.

5. **Public Awareness:** With the advent of mass media and, later, the internet, global events and environmental crises became more visible. This increased public awareness and pressure on countries and institutions to prioritize preservation.

Over the past century, the convergence of industrial consequences, visible species decline, enhanced scientific understanding, international collaboration, and public awareness have thrust wildlife conservation into the spotlight.

Endangered Species List: From Inception to Now

The Endangered Species List came into prominence with the U.S. Endangered Species Act of 1973. This groundbreaking act sought to safeguard and rescue imperiled species and their environments. Initially, the list focused primarily on species within the U.S. and its territories.

Today, the scope has expanded significantly. Modern efforts recognize a more significant number of endangered species globally and integrate advanced scientific methods, technology, and international cooperation to assess threats and implement conservation strategies. The list's evolution reflects our growing understanding of biodiversity's global interconnectedness and wildlife's escalating challenges.

Large Mammals on the Brink: The Rescue Stories of African Rhinoceroses and American Bison

Large mammals face heightened extinction risks due to habitat loss, hunting, and slower reproduction rates. African rhinos, targeted for their horns, saw catastrophic population declines. However, African private reserves, backed by individuals and NGOs, have made significant strides in anti-poaching and conservation efforts, helping rhino numbers recover.

Similarly, the American bison faced near-extinction due to overhunting. Passionate individuals and ranchers initiated private breeding programs, playing a pivotal role in restoring bison populations. These stories underscore the power of individual action in reversing the dire fates of endangered large mammals.

Wildlife Conservation: The Evolution from Individuals to Modern Strategies

Historically, private individuals spearheaded wildlife conservation. Over time, NGOs emerged, leveraging collective resources and expertise for a more significant impact. An example is the European bison. After near-extinction due to hunting and habitat loss, concerted efforts by NGOs and governments have revived their numbers.

The 1990s saw the U.S. develop Safe Harbor agreements, incentivizing landowners to take conservation actions on their properties. This partnership model recognized the integral function of private grounds in conservation.

The Airbnb wildlife concept emerged as a novel approach, blending tourism and conservation. By letting travelers experience wildlife in natural habitats, it raises awareness while generating funds for conservation.

Graeme Caughly, a prominent ecologist, tragically died in 1994. His passing shifted wildlife conservation focus more toward rescue efforts. Caughly's work was pivotal in population dynamics, emphasizing sustainable wildlife management.

While rescue is vital, it's essential to understand that isolated rescue efforts alone don't curb extinction rates. Addressing the root causes—habitat destruction, climate change, and human-wildlife conflict—is crucial. Solely rescuing animals without considering the broader ecosystem fails to create sustainable solutions.

While individual efforts laid conservation's foundation, contemporary strategies recognize the necessity of holistic approaches and diverse collaborations.

The Technological Dilemma: Balancing Benefits and Risks in Species Preservation

The rapid progression of technology has presented humanity with both incredible opportunities and significant ethical dilemmas, especially in fields like biology and conservation. In vitro fertilization (IVF) is a prime example of this double-edged sword. While it offers potential solutions to problems like declining species numbers, it also raises questions about the limits and implications of our intervention.

Pros of Using Technology like IVF

1. **Species Revival:** Technologies like IVF can provide a lifeline for critically endangered species. Collecting and preserving genetic material can restore a species even after its natural population has dwindled.
2. **Genetic Diversity:** IVF allows scientists to strategically select genetic material to maximize genetic diversity, ensuring a healthy and resilient future population.
3. **Overcome Natural Limitations:** For species that face breeding challenges, whether due to environmental changes, human interference, or inherent issues, IVF can bypass these barriers and increase the chances of successful reproduction.

Cons of Using Technology like IVF

1. **Ethical Concerns:** Intervening in the natural reproductive process might be seen as playing god. Questions arise about the rights of the animals and the long-term implications of such interventions.
2. **Loss of Natural Behaviors:** Relying on technology might mean certain species lose inherent reproductive behaviors, which could have broader implications for survival and adaptation.

3. **Resource Intensive:** Technologies like IVF are expensive and require technical tools and expertise. Allocating resources to these methods diverts them from other conservation strategies.

Case of the Sumatran Rhino

The Sumatran rhino stands as a pertinent example of this debate. With a significantly decreased birth rate and fewer than eighty individuals left in the wild by 2022, their survival hangs in the balance.

- **What Happened?** Over the years, the Sumatran rhino faced hazards from a naturally low birth rate, poaching for their horns, and habitat loss. The fragmented populations further decreased their chances of natural reproduction.
- **Why Technology Might Be Their Last Hope:** Given their dire numbers and the challenges they face in breeding, technological interventions like IVF have become crucial. There have been efforts to create rhino embryos using IVF, aiming to implant them in surrogate mothers. This increases their numbers and guarantees genetic diversity, which is critical for long-term survival.
- **The Ongoing Debate:** While technology offers hope, it's a solution that some people believe should be approached with caution. There's a fear that an over-reliance on IVF may make us complacent about habitat restoration and anti-poaching efforts. After all, the

best chance for any species' survival is in its natural habitat.

While the allure of technology in species conservation is strong, it's essential to balance it with ethical considerations and a holistic approach to protection. The case of the Sumatran rhino underscores the urgency of the situation and the delicate tightrope we walk between intervention and preservation.

The Evolution of Science: From Natural History Observations to Data-Driven Multidisciplinary Studies

Over the past eighty years, how we approach and discuss science has radically transformed. The fast rise of technology and the increasing importance of data-driven methods are at the heart of this change.

1. **From Observational to Quantitative:** In the early twentieth century, natural history and observational field studies were the basis of science. Researchers would spend vast amounts of time documenting nature's species, behaviors, and environmental interactions. While these studies provided valuable insights, the scope of human observation and the tools available at the time often limited them.

2. **Rise of Technology:** As technology advanced, particularly in the latter half of the twentieth century, it introduced a range of new tools for scientists. From advanced microscopy to satellite imaging and computer simulations to genetic sequencing, these technological

innovations allowed scientists to explore the natural world in previously unimaginable ways.

3. **Data at the Forefront:** With the proliferation of technology, vast amounts of data began to accumulate. This necessitated the development of data analysis methods and tools. Suddenly, being a scientist wasn't just about observing and hypothesizing; it was about analyzing complex datasets, identifying patterns, and making predictions.

4. **A Multidisciplinary Approach:** The increasing complexity of scientific questions meant that no single discipline could answer them alone. As a result, science has become more collaborative and interdisciplinary. Bioinformatics, for example, merges biology and computer science to understand complex genetic data. Similarly, climate science today requires expertise in meteorology, oceanography, geology, and even sociology to provide comprehensive solutions.

5. **Applied Science Takes Center Stage:** With this newfound ability to gather and analyze data, science has become more applied. Instead of just understanding the world, there's a growing emphasis on using this understanding to solve real-world problems. Whether developing new medical treatments, creating sustainable energy solutions, or tackling climate change, today's science is about applying knowledge to improve society.

The last eighty years have shifted from purely observational studies rooted in natural history to a more multifaceted, data-driven approach. Today, science is about observing the world, understanding its intricate patterns, and leveraging that understanding to create positive change.

KEY TAKEAWAYS

- Wildlife conservation protects plant and animal species in natural habitats to preserve biodiversity and maintain ecological balance.
- The immediate objective is to ensure the survival and well-being of species and their habitats, recognizing their interconnectedness within ecosystems.
- Conservation methods include habitat conservation, sustainable land-use practices, research, public education, wildlife area creation, recycling, legal protection, physical protection, species management, reintroduction, genetic storage, invasive species control, captive breeding and rescue, rehabilitation, and release.
- The Endangered Species List has expanded to protect imperiled species worldwide, reflecting a growing understanding of global biodiversity.
- Large mammals like African rhinos and American bison have experienced population recoveries due to preservation measures.
- Technology like in vitro fertilization (IVF) presents opportunities and ethical dilemmas in species preservation.

- Data-driven and multidisciplinary approaches have transformed the field of science, allowing for more comprehensive and applied solutions to real-world problems.

Now that we've explored the evolution and various aspects of wildlife conservation, let's delve into the fundamental principles of conservation science in the next chapter.

2

CONSERVATION SCIENCE

> *"If we can teach people about wildlife, they will be touched. Share my wildlife with me. Because humans want to save things that they love."*
>
> — *STEVE IRWIN*

Steve Irwin, the renowned Crocodile Hunter, emphasized the profound connection between understanding and affection for wildlife. When we truly know and appreciate the intricate lives of surrounding creatures, our inherent desire to protect them grows stronger. This deep connection to wildlife underscores the importance of academic disciplines dedicated to their preservation.

One might wonder, however, about the nuances between fields like Conservation Science and Conservation Biology. Although they might seem synonymous to the uninitiated, they each have distinct focuses and methodologies. Let's understand the distinctions between these two critical areas of study.

THE CONTRAST BETWEEN CONSERVATION BIOLOGY AND CONSERVATION SCIENCE

Conservation science and biology aim to protect ecosystems but approach this goal differently. While they share common ground, understanding their differences is crucial for practical environmental preservation.

Conservation Science

Conservation science is an interdisciplinary field that blends knowledge from various disciplines, such as biology, ecology, social sciences, and economics. Its primary objective is to furnish a scientific foundation for protecting and managing biodiversity and ecosystems.

This discipline takes a broad view, addressing practical issues like designing protected areas, managing species populations, and mitigating threats like habitat loss and climate change. Conservation science integrates biological and human factors, ensuring strategies and policies are grounded in thorough research and understanding.

Conservation Biology

Conservation biology, often dubbed a "crisis discipline," has an acute sense of urgency. While other scientific endeavors might be purely exploratory, conservation biology operates under the premise that rapid action is essential to prevent biodiversity loss.

This gives it a unique position in the scientific community: while it's grounded in empirical research, its primary focus is developing and implementing immediate solutions to pressing environmental problems.

The label "crisis discipline" underscores this difference. Many fields of study prioritize understanding, theorizing, and knowledge accumulation, often over extended periods. In contrast, conservation biology is driven by the immediate need to halt or reverse declines in biodiversity. This urgency necessitates swift decision-making, often with incomplete data, making it distinct from other scientific endeavors.

Conservation Science and Conservation Biology: Two Sides of the Same Coin

While conservation science and biology have nuanced differences, they share many similarities and ultimately converge in their goals.

1. **Shared Objective:** Both fields are anchored in the mission to preserve biodiversity and ensure the health and longevity of ecosystems. They recognize the intrinsic value of the natural world and work to safeguard it against its myriad threats.

2. **Empirical Basis:** Both disciplines prioritize a rigorous scientific approach. They use data collection, analysis, and empirical evidence to inform their recommendations and actions. This emphasis on evidence-based decision-making sets them apart from less structured or anecdotal conservation efforts.

3. **Practical Solutions:** Both conservation science and biology are oriented toward developing actionable solutions to contemporary challenges. Whether designing wildlife corridors, restoring habitats, or creating conservation policies, the focus is always on tangible, real-world impact.

4. **Interdisciplinary Collaboration:** Recognizing that conservation issues are multifaceted, both fields often involve collaboration with experts from other disciplines. This may include economists, sociologists, or policymakers, ensuring a holistic approach to conservation.

In an era where biodiversity is under unprecedented threat, the roles of conservation science and conservation biology are paramount. Both fields bring a scientific rigor to the realm of wildlife conservation.

By prioritizing data collection, they ensure conservation efforts are well-intentioned and effective. They offer methodologies to address modern challenges, from habitat fragmentation to climate change, grounding their strategies in evidence and research.

While the nuances between conservation science and conservation biology are worth noting, their shared commitment to preserving the natural world stands out. Both offer structured, scientific frameworks to approach wildlife conservation, ensuring that efforts are passionate but also pragmatic and practical.

While conservation science and conservation biology provide the scientific framework for wildlife preservation, it's important to understand how external factors, such as major donors and corporations, influence and steer the course of conservation efforts.

HOW DONORS AND CORPORATIONS SHAPE CONSERVATION GOALS

Major corporations and large foundations have increasingly become key players in conservation funding. Their massive financial clout means their donations can significantly influence the direction and priorities of conservation organizations. However, this influx of funds isn't without its complications.

The Gates' Impact on Conservation International

The Bill and Melinda Gates Foundation, known primarily for its health and education initiatives, donated $10 million to Conservation International in 2012. The impact of this donation was transformative. It brought a substantial financial boost and garnered attention from other potential donors. The funds enabled Conservation International to expand its programs, initiate new research projects, and enhance its conservation efforts on a global scale.

The Shift in Conservation Missions

Conservation organizations have pivoted their mission statements and strategies to appeal to big corporations and major foundations. This shift often characterizes a transition from a strictly wildlife-centric approach to a more human-centric one, sometimes called "new conservation." The rationale behind this shift is that conservation outcomes are more achievable when they also factor in human well-being, economic development, and sustainability.

Institutions like the World Wildlife Fund (WWF) and The Nature Conservancy (TNC) have, to varying degrees, integrated this broader approach into their missions. By aligning conservation goals with general socio-economic objectives, these organizations hope to attract donors who view conservation as a noble endeavor and a strategic investment.

The Donor Game: The Moore Foundation's Approach

The Gordon and Betty Moore Foundation is another significant player in the conservation funding landscape. It has at least a $6 billion endowment. Their donations, often sizable, come with specific stipulations on how to allocate the funds. For instance, the Moore Foundation donated $395 million to Conservation International over the span of ten years. It committed $100 million over five years to establish new protected areas and manage existing ones in the Amazon and Andes regions of South America.

The foundation announced $90 million dedicated to improving the sustainability of food production, aligning with the principles of new conservation efforts. It also has shown interest in funding cattle efficiency to reduce deforestation.

While such an approach has merits, it has also led to controversies. Some conservationists argue that the foundation's influence diverts attention from other pressing conservation issues. Moreover, specific organizations with differing goals have found it challenging to collaborate with the foundation, given its particular focus areas.

From Individuals to Corporate Giants

Historically, conservation organizations relied heavily on individual donors and grassroots support. However, as the challenges facing our planet have grown in magnitude, the financial needs of these organizations have skyrocketed. With their vast resources, big corporations and foundations fill this funding gap. Their influence on setting agendas and priorities has grown proportionally.

The Unfortunate Underdogs of Conservation Funding

While charismatic megafauna like tigers, elephants, and pandas often attract substantial funding, many lesser-known species remain underfunded. Despite facing significant threats, animals like pangolins and sharks often struggle to secure the financial support they need. The reasons are multifaceted: these animals may lack the "cute" factor, or their conservation might not align with corporate interests or strategies.

Why Big Corporations Hold the Reins

Big corporations influence conservation funding in several ways:

1. Their donations often come with strings attached, shaping the direction of the recipient organization's work.
2. Their involvement can inspire other entities to donate, creating a multiplier effect.
3. Corporations have the resources to fund large-scale projects or initiatives that individual donors may need help to support.

However, this influence is a double-edged sword. On the one hand, corporate involvement brings much-needed funds and attention to conservation efforts. On the other, it risks narrowing the focus of conservation to areas that align with corporate interests, potentially sidelining other critical issues.

The landscape of conservation funding has evolved dramatically, with major corporations and foundations playing an increasingly prominent role. While their involvement has undeniably accelerated many conservation efforts, ensuring a balance is essential. Conservation should remain a holistic endeavor, addressing famous and less glamorous causes and ensuring that the planet's biodiversity is preserved for generations.

The UN's Global Biodiversity Framework has acted as a catalyst, pushing forward research in genetic variation. By emphasizing the importance of genetic diversity in the broader conservation agenda, the Framework has paved the way for a more comprehensive and nuanced approach to preserving our planet's rich biological tapestry.

The Royal Zoological Society of Scotland (RZSS) has made significant advancements in conservation efforts for the critically endangered dama gazelle, utilizing genetic research. RZSS's WildGenes laboratory scientists have been working with international partners to create this species' first comprehensive genetic study.

By analyzing genetic samples from both wild and zoo populations, the team aims to better understand the dama gazelle's genetic diversity and distribution. This research will provide essential insights, aiding in making informed decisions about the management and reintroduction programs for the species.

The ultimate goal is to bolster the dama gazelle's numbers and ensure its long-term survival in the wild.

GENETIC VARIATION AND THE CONNECTION TO POPULATION SIZE

Genetic variation is the foundation upon which the health and survival of animal populations rest. Understanding its significance, mechanisms, and impacts can guide more effective conservation strategies, ensuring the longevity of various species in the face of ever-changing environmental challenges.

Understanding Genetic Variation

At its core, genetic variation refers to the discrepancies in DNA sequences among individuals within a population. These differences arise from mutations, gene flow, and the shuffling of genes during reproduction. This genetic diversity is essential because it supplies the raw material upon which natural selection can act, enabling populations to adapt to their environments and respond to evolving challenges.

Consequences of Low Genetic Variation

Populations with low genetic variation face several threats. First, they are more susceptible to diseases, as there's a lack of diversity in immune response genes. Second, reduced genetic diversity can lead to inbreeding, in which closely related individuals breed, often resulting in offspring with health problems.

Moreover, once a population experiences a dramatic loss in genetic variation, even if its size subsequently increases, the level of genetic diversity doesn't rebound as quickly. This is particularly concerning for endangered species, as they may risk extinction even after their population has ostensibly recovered.

Genetic Theory and Population Size

A well-established genetic theory states that genetic variation should increase with adequate population size. Larger populations have more potential for mutations and genetic mixing, resulting in more significant genetic diversity. In contrast, smaller populations are more vulnerable to genetic drift, where the frequency of particular genes changes purely by chance, reducing genetic diversity.

The Promise of Genetic Rescue

Genetic rescue involves introducing individuals from genetically diverse populations into populations with low genetic diversity. This can boost the genetic health of the latter population, increasing its chances of survival and adaptability. Despite its potential, few studies have attempted genetic tracking in wildlife populations to facilitate this method.

A compelling case study illustrating the benefits of adding new genes to a population involves a specific fish species. The population witnessed a ten-fold increase upon introducing new genes, and its genetic diversity doubled. Notably, this led to the elimination of pure residents, ensuring a healthy mix of genes in the population.

When Genetic Rescue Can Be Counterproductive

However, genetic rescue isn't a panacea. There are instances where introducing new genes can backfire. The case of the island foxes offers a cautionary tale. These foxes exhibited a high risk of cancer, and introducing new genes could have exacerbated this risk. In such cases, letting nature take its course might be more prudent than intervening with genetic rescue.

Genetic variation plays an irreplaceable role in the health and adaptability of animal populations. While strategies like genetic rescue offer promising solutions to counter the threats of low genetic diversity, they must be employed judiciously, considering each species' unique challenges and needs.

As we forge ahead in our conservation endeavors, a nuanced understanding of genetic principles will be indispensable in safeguarding the myriad species that call our planet home.

THE CLASSIFICATION OF ANIMALS: TAXONOMY

The classification of animals, or taxonomy, systematically organizes Earth's diverse species based on shared traits, offering insights into evolutionary relationships and aiding scientific understanding.

What Is Animal Classification?

Animal classification, or taxonomy, is the scientific method of arranging and classifying living organisms based on shared attributes. This system aids in understanding the vast diversity of life on Earth, allowing for a more explicit depiction of relationships between different organisms.

The modern framework for animal classification owes its inception to Carolus Linnaeus, a renowned Swedish botanist from the eighteenth century. Linnaeus developed a structured system to name, describe, and categorize species, simplifying the once chaotic vocabulary of the animal kingdom. His innovative approach, grounded in observation and meticulous categorization, laid the bedrock for today's taxonomy.

By introducing binomial nomenclature, Linnaeus provided a standardized way to name organisms. This system, which assigns each species a two-part Latin name (the first part representing the genus and the second the species), ensures that every species has a unique and universally recognized name.

Linnaeus's contributions to animal classification provided a structured lens through which we can comprehend the intricate web of life, making sense of the myriad species that inhabit our planet.

Nine Branches of Biological Classification

Biological classification offers a structured way to organize the immense diversity of life on Earth. By categorizing living organisms based on shared characteristics, we can better understand evolutionary relationships and the intricate interplay of life. Let's delve into the nine branching categories that form the backbone of this classification system:

1. **Domain:** This is the most general category. Organisms fall under three domains based on cell types and specific molecular characteristics: Bacteria (prokaryotic microorganisms), Archaea (prokaryotes often found in extreme environments), and Eukarya (organisms with eukaryotic cells, including humans). Example: Humans belong to the Eukarya domain.

2. **Kingdom:** Within domains, we further classify organisms into kingdoms. Historically, we had two kingdoms: Animalia and Plantae. However, multiple kingdoms like Fungi, Protista, and Eubacteria emerged with our advancements in understanding. Example: Pine trees fall under the Plantae kingdom.

3. **Phylum:** This category differentiates organisms based on major structural and functional characteristics. For instance, in the Animalia kingdom, distinctions like the presence of a backbone can lead to different phyla. Example: Butterflies belong to the Arthropoda phylum.

4. **Class:** Within a phylum, organisms fall under different classes based on further specific characteristics.

Example*:* With their feathered bodies, birds are under the Aves class.

5. **Order:** Orders further divide the class, grouping organisms with more specific traits. Example*:* Cats, being carnivorous mammals, fall under the Carnivora order.

6. **Suborder:** This category refines the order further, focusing on more nuanced shared attributes. Example*:* Placental mammals, like humans, are part of the Placentalia suborder.

7. **Animal Families:** Families group species based on particular shared traits closer to suborders. Example*:* Given its characteristics and lineage, the domestic dog is a part of the Canidae family.

8. **Genus:** One step above species, the genus clusters closely related species and share a common ancestor. Example*: Felis catus,* or the house cat, belongs to the *Felis* genus.

9. **Species:** The most specific classification level is that of individuals that can interbreed and beget fertile descendants under natural circumstances. Example*:* Humans are *Homo sapiens,* where "*sapiens*" denotes our species.

These nine branches, from domain to species, provide a comprehensive roadmap to the complexity of life. Walking through each category gives us a clearer perspective on the evolutionary relationships and shared characteristics that bind the living world.

Unveiling the Six Kingdoms of Life

The diversity of life on Earth is immense, and to make sense of this vast array of organisms, scientists have divided them into six distinct kingdoms. Each kingdom represents a significant category of life based on unique sets of characteristics. Let's journey through these six kingdoms:

1. Animal Kingdom (Animalia)

- **Characteristics:** The animal kingdom consists of multicellular, eukaryotic organisms that are typically mobile at some stage in their life cycle. They obtain nutrients by consuming organic substances, whether plant or animal.
- **Example:** Lions, elephants, and humans are all part of the Animal kingdom.

2. Plant Kingdom (Plantae)

- **Characteristics:** The plant kingdom consists of multicellular, eukaryotic organisms that use photosynthesis to produce food. They have cell walls made of cellulose.
- **Example:** From the tall redwood trees to the daisies in your garden, they all fall under the Plant kingdom.

WILDLIFE CONSERVATION DECODED | 51

3. Fungi Kingdom

- **Characteristics:** The fungi kingdom has eukaryotic organisms that are neither flora nor fauna. They absorb nutrients from decomposed organic matter, possessing cell walls made of chitin.
- **Example:** Mushrooms on the forest floor and the yeast used in bread-making are representatives of the Fungi kingdom.

4. Protista Kingdom

- **Characteristics:** A diverse group of eukaryotic microorganisms, Protista includes organisms that don't fit neatly into other kingdoms. They can be single-celled or simple multicellular organisms. Modes of nutrition can be autotrophic (like plants) or heterotrophic (like animals).
- **Example:** The amoeba, a single-celled organism found in pond water, is part of the Protista kingdom.

5. Eubacteria Kingdom

- **Characteristics:** These are single-celled prokaryotic organisms, indicating they don't have a nucleus. Eubacteria are incredibly diverse and can exist in many environments, from the human gut to the ocean's deepest trenches.

- **Example:** The Lactobacillus bacteria found in yogurt, known for its probiotic properties, belongs to the Eubacteria kingdom.

6. Archaebacteria Kingdom (Archaea)

- **Characteristics:** Archaebacteria are a group of single-celled microorganisms. They are distinct from bacteria and share similarities with both bacteria and eukaryotes but belong to a separate domain of life. They have the ability to thrive in extreme environments, such as hot springs, deep-sea hydrothermal vents, and acidic lakes.
- **Example:** Methanogens, a type of Archaea, play a crucial role in anaerobic environments, such as the digestive tracts of animals, by producing methane gas.

These six kingdoms encapsulate our planet's myriad life forms, from the tallest trees to the tiniest microbes. Through this classification system, we can appreciate the evolutionary marvels and adaptations that have enabled life to flourish in nearly every corner of the Earth.

A Deep Dive into Animal Phyla

The animal kingdom is an astonishing tapestry of diversity, hosting creatures of every imaginable shape, size, and function. Scientists have classified animals into phyla (singular: phylum) based on fundamental structural and developmental differences to better understand this vast expanse of life. Here are some intriguing phyla:

1. Porifera (Simple and Primitive Aquatic Animals)

- **Characteristics:** Simple multicellular organisms, sponges have porous bodies and lack actual tissues or organs. They sift feed by allowing liquids through their bodies and removing nutrients.
- **Example:** The bath sponge, once a living organism, is a well-known representative of this phylum.

2. Cnidaria (Aquatic Animals with Radial Symmetry)

- **Characteristics:** Characterized by radial symmetry, cnidarians possess specialized cells called cnidocytes, which contain stinging structures for defense and capturing prey.
- **Example:** The moon jellyfish, with its delicate, translucent body, belongs to the Cnidaria phylum.

3. Platyhelminthes (Simple Body without a Cavity)

- **Characteristics:** As their name suggests, these are flat-bodied worms. They have a simple body plan without a cavity and include many parasitic forms.
- **Example:** The tapeworm, which can reside in the intestines of various animals, including humans, is a member of this phylum.

4. Annelida (Segmented Body with a Fluid-Filled Cavity)

- **Characteristics:** These worms have segmented bodies. They have a fluid-filled cavity known as the celom.
- **Example:** Earthworms, commonly found in gardens and known for their role in enriching soil, are part of the Annelida phylum.

5. Mollusca (Hard Shell with Soft Body)

- **Characteristics:** Mollusks typically have a soft body, often protected by a hard shell. They have a visceral mass and a distinctive head and foot.
- **Example:** The garden snail, with its spiral shell and slow movement, is a recognizable member of the Mollusca phylum.

6. Arthropoda (Segmented Body with Jointed Limbs)

- **Characteristics:** This is the most extensive phylum in the animal kingdom. Arthropods have jointed limbs, segmented bodies, and an exoskeleton made of chitin that they must shed to grow.
- **Example:** The monarch butterfly, admired for its striking orange and black wings and the common house spider hail from the Arthropoda phylum.

7. Chordata (Vertebrates with Gill Slits and a Dorsal Concave Nerve Cord)

- **Characteristics:** Chordates have gill slits, a dorsal concave nerve cord, and a notochord at some point in their life. This phylum includes animals with backbones (vertebrates) and a few without.
- **Example:** Humans, with our complex skeletal structure, are members of the Chordata phylum, as are blue whales and hummingbirds.

These phyla offer a structured view into the vast world of animals, each showcasing unique evolutionary adaptations that have enabled them to thrive in various environments across our planet. Whether you're marveling at the fluttering of a butterfly or the intricate design of a coral, you're witnessing the wonders of the diverse animal phyla.

KEY TAKEAWAYS

- Conservation Science is interdisciplinary, addressing practical issues like designing protected areas and mitigating threats, integrating biological and human factors.
- Conservation Biology operates urgently, focusing on immediate solutions to prevent biodiversity loss.
- Major corporations and foundations, like the Bill and Melinda Gates Foundation and the Gordon and Betty

Moore Foundation, significantly impact conservation funding.

- Genetic variation is crucial for the health and survival of animal populations.
- Low genetic diversity can lead to susceptibility to diseases and inbreeding.
- Animal classification, or taxonomy, organizes species based on shared characteristics.
- Biological classification includes domains, kingdoms, phyla, classes, orders, families, genera, and species.
- The six kingdoms of life are Animalia, Plantae, Fungi, Protista, Eubacteria, and Archaebacteria.
- Animal phyla categorize creatures based on structural and developmental differences.
- Each phylum represents diverse evolutionary transformations that allow species to flourish in many conditions.

Now that we have explored the key concepts in conservation science, genetics, and animal classification, let's discuss the crucial topic of biodiversity and discover its significance in our natural world.

3

DISCOVERING THE IMPORTANCE OF BIODIVERSITY

66 *"The value of biodiversity is that it makes our ecosystems more resilient, which is a prerequisite for stable societies; its wanton destruction is akin to setting fire to our lifeboat."*

— *JOHAN ROCKSTROM*

Biodiversity is the bedrock of healthy ecosystems. The variety of life forms, from tiny microorganisms to towering trees, all play interconnected roles that maintain ecological balance. A diverse ecosystem can better withstand external shocks, ensuring the sustained provision of essential services like clean air, fresh water, and food. Stable ecosystems, in turn, provide the foundation for human societies to flourish.

Johan Rockstrom's analogy of "setting fire to our lifeboat" underscores the self-destructive nature of heedlessly destroying biodiversity. Without this natural wealth, our survival systems become vulnerable, risking societal collapse. Hence, safeguarding biodiversity is not just an ecological concern but a socio-economic imperative.

To truly grasp the gravity of our actions and their consequences on the environment, we must first discuss the concept of biodiversity and understand its paramount significance in the web of life.

UNDERSTANDING BIODIVERSITY AND ITS IMPORTANCE

Biodiversity, encompassing the vast spectrum of life on Earth, is integral to ecosystem health and stability. Appreciating its significance not only deepens our connection to nature but underscores the urgent need to safeguard this invaluable treasure for present and future generations.

What Is Biodiversity?

Biodiversity includes all life forms on Earth, consisting of flora and fauna. Out of an estimated 8.7 million species, only 1.2 million have been identified, with insects dominating this count (*Biodiversity*, 2023). Biodiversity studies focus on global diversity and within specific ecosystems, like grasslands and tropical regions.

Areas such as Mexico, South Africa, and Madagascar are rich biodiversity hotspots with unique endemic species. Every species plays a role in ecosystem health, providing resources like food and medicine for humans. However, human-induced challenges like pollution and climate change are accelerating extinction rates. Intensified conservation efforts are imperative to protect our planet's rich biodiversity.

The Importance of Biodiversity

Biodiversity is pivotal in our lives, offering practical benefits and intrinsic worth. From a practical standpoint, biodiversity supplies fundamental resources like food, energy, shelter, and medication. Ecosystems offer vital support to agriculture such as seed dispersal, climate stabilization, water cleansing, nutrient recycling, and pest regulation.

Moreover, there's a potential for undiscovered benefits, possibly new medicines or unknown ecological functions. Culturally, many societies cherish biodiversity for its spiritual or religious significance. Inherently, biodiversity possesses a value independent of its utility and has a fundamental right to exist.

Our relationship with biodiversity shapes our identities, connections, and societal standards, emphasizing the shared bond and responsibility we have towards our environment. Recognizing these diverse values of biodiversity is crucial, as they inform the daily conservation choices we make.

Biodiversity and Species Richness

Biodiversity often brings to mind the concept of species rich-ness, which counts the number of unique species in a given area. By analyzing species richness, we gain insights into the ecological variations across regions.

For instance, the Amazon rainforest boasts an impressive diversity with over 116,000 known species, encompassing more than 14,000 types of flowering plants and over 5,500 vertebrates. On the other hand, the Sahara Desert has significantly less diversity, hosting perhaps only around 500 plant and 300 vertebrate species (Pavid, n.d.).

While scientists have documented about 1.7 million species, predominantly insects, they believe countless others remain undiscovered on our planet (Pavid, n.d.).

The ocean's vastness also harbors diverse life forms, like the myriad deep-sea fishes. It's widely believed that many marine creatures still await discovery.

With such a rich tapestry of life coloring our planet, it becomes imperative to address the looming challenges. Let's delve into the threats facing biodiversity and understand the urgency to act in its defense.

THREATS TO BIODIVERSITY

Biodiversity, the mixture of living things on Earth, faces unprecedented threats. From climate change to invasive species, these challenges not only endanger countless species but also threaten the intricate balance of our planet's ecosystems and the vital services they provide.

Declining Biodiversity

To provide some context: North America has seen a staggering loss of three billion birds since 1970, while beetle populations in the United States have plummeted by 83 percent in the past four decades. Currently, 41 percent of U.S. ecosystems teeter on the brink of widespread collapse (*5 Threats To Biodiversity and How We Can Counter Them*, 2023). Additionally, in 2020, the World Economic Forum identified biodiversity loss as a significant risk to the global economic landscape.

Five Threats to Biodiversity

Biodiversity underpins the health of our planet, but it faces significant threats. Here, we spotlight five primary challenges: climate change, overexploitation of species, pollution, habitat loss, and invasive species, each playing a pivotal role in shaping the future of global ecosystems.

Climate Change

Climate change, potentially raising global temperatures by over 1.5 °C by 2030, increasingly threatens biodiversity. Worsened by climate shifts, fires like those in Australia from 2019 to 2020 decimated habitats and likely increased threatened species by 14 percent. Elevated temperatures also reshape ecosystems, with recent data showing 59 percent of global vegetated areas undergoing browning since the 1990s (*How Does Climate Change Affect Biodiversity*, n.d.).

Marine life struggles with warmer waters and acidification, affecting corals and shellfish. On a hopeful note, ecosystems like mangroves effectively store carbon, and the Amazon holds nearly 100 billion tons of it (*How Does Climate Change Affect Biodiversity*, n.d.). Prioritizing the protection of these carbon-rich habitats is essential to combating climate change.

Overexploitation of Species

In the past fifty years, significant ecological changes have put nearly a million species on the brink of extinction and imperiled crucial ecosystem services like disease control and pollination. Human behaviors primarily cause this decline, resulting in habitat changes, climate change, pollution, and invasive species.

For instance, historical overhunting led to the extinction of mammoths, the dodo, Steller's sea cow, the passenger pigeon, and the massive decline of sea otter populations. The passenger pigeon, once North America's most populous bird, became extinct by 1914 due to overhunting (*Drivers of Biodiversity Loss: Overexploitation*, 2022).

The sea otter, valued for its dense fur, saw its numbers dwindle drastically by the mid-nineteenth century, with only thirteen small populations remaining. A 1911 treaty began global wildlife protection efforts (*Drivers of Biodiversity Loss: Overexploitation*, 2022).

Though Californian sea otters have seen some recovery, they still face numerous threats, including toxoplasmosis and oil spills. Their loss profoundly affected the biodiversity of Pacific coastal ecosystems.

Pollution

Air pollution damages ecosystems and reduces biodiversity. Ground-level ozone hinders plant growth and impacts biodiversity. Pollutants like nitrogen oxides and ammonia introduce excess nitrogen, causing aquatic eutrophication and oxygen reduction. On land, excessive nitrogen can lead to species loss and ecosystem imbalance.

Sulfur dioxide, along with nitrogen oxide and ammonia, acidifies soils and waters, harming biodiversity. The EEA emphasized in 2019 that, with declining sulfur dioxide emissions, ammonia and nitrogen oxide have become primary acidifying agents (*Impacts of Air Pollution on Ecosystems*, 2022). Additionally, heavy metals in the atmosphere, when settled, accumulate in ecosystems and cause bioaccumulation and biomagnification, posing further threats.

Habitat Loss

Wildlife faces urgent threats, necessitating immediate conservation actions. From the 2020 World Wildlife Fund's endangered list:

1. **Indian Elephants:** Central to Indian culture, they face habitat loss from human expansion, resulting in food and shelter scarcity.
2. **Whales:** Of the North Atlantic whales, a mere 400 remain. Shipping routes overlap their habitats, causing ship strikes, gear entanglements, and pollution-related harm.

3. **Mountain Gorillas:** Approximately 1,000 inhabit central Africa, endangered by agriculture, livestock farming, poaching, and charcoal production, especially in Virunga National Park.

4. **Black Rhinoceros:** Of this African species, 5,600 survive, threatened by horn poaching and habitat encroachment.

5. **Sea Turtles:** Having existed for 100 million years, they now face risks from coastal development, pollution, climate change, overfishing, and illegal trade.

6. **Orangutans:** Over half reside outside protected zones due to illegal logging and oil palm plantation expansion.

7. **Red Pandas:** Native to the Eastern Himalayas, they're endangered by the loss of nesting trees and bamboo.

8. **Tigers:** Despite some population stability, Southeast Asia's tigers face habitat reduction from agriculture, logging, and urbanization.

9. **African Wild Dogs:** Threatened by hunting, diseases, predators, and diminishing habitats from human population growth (Bennett, 2020).

Many endangered species grapple with habitat decline, human interference, and direct endangerment, emphasizing the critical need for conservation measures.

Invasive Species

Invasive alien species, introduced to new areas, often flourish and disrupt local biodiversity, health, and economies. They can prey on native species, alter habitats, compete for resources, interbreed, and introduce diseases.

Although not all introduced species become invasive, some transmit diseases, provoke allergies, or produce toxins that affect human health and sectors like fisheries, agriculture, and tourism. Notably, many domesticated animals and crops, such as potatoes and corn, coexist without harm in their adopted habitats.

Primary human-linked introductions include:

1. **Wildlife Trade:** The foremost cause, with the illegal trade valued at around 10 billion dollars yearly, according to WWF (*Stop Wildlife Crime*, n.d.).
2. **Tourism:** International travel inadvertently promotes the spread of non-native species.
3. **Recreational Hunting and Fishing:** Past activities introduced species like barbary sheep and catfish in Europe.
4. **Global Transport:** Species often stow away in aircraft cargoes, shipping containers, or on ships.
5. **Pets:** Animals like cats and red-eared slider turtles, once domesticated, now thrive after escaping or being released.
6. **Agriculture and Fur Trade:** The fashion and horticultural industries have inadvertently spread species globally.

It's essential to address these introduction pathways and manage invasive species proactively to protect native ecosystems and human well-being.

Understanding these threats is crucial, as they impact biodiversity on several levels: ecosystem, species, and genetic. Exploring further, we'll discuss how each level faces unique challenges yet is interconnected in maintaining the delicate balance of our natural world.

THE THREE BIODIVERSITY LEVELS

Biodiversity includes all life on Earth, spanning three primary levels: ecosystem, species, and genetic diversity. Each level offers distinctive insights into the richness and complexity of our planet's biological resources, highlighting the complex interaction between organisms and their habitats.

Genetic Diversity

Genetic diversity reflects the variety within genes, which are composed of DNA. These genes dictate an organism's characteristics and functions. Diversity can range from allele gene variants like eye colors to whole genes that determine specific traits and even broader structures like chromosomes.

The scope of genetic diversity can span various levels: population, species, community, or biome. The level of choice depends on the study's focus, but its value stays constant.

Why Does It Matter?

Genetic diversity serves as the foundation for evolution and adaptability. A species or population with rich genetic diversity possesses a heightened capacity to adjust to environmental shifts. In contrast, limited diversity results in uniformity, restricting adaptability to evolving conditions.

For instance, while monocultures in agriculture (large fields of genetically identical crops) aid in streamlined cultivation, they are vulnerable to diseases, as every plant shares the same susceptibility. Their adaptability to changing scenarios is also compromised.

What Is Its Relevance?

Within a species, fluctuating environments often correspond with increased genetic diversity. Frequent environmental changes mean that various genes offer advantages at distinct times, maintaining a high genetic diversity. A stable environment, however, might promote the dominance of a few advantageous genes, diminishing overall diversity.

In community ecosystems, species diversity can influence genetic diversity. The genetic contribution varies depending on the species' relatedness. For instance, closely related species, like two maple types, share genetic similarities and add limited genetic diversity. In contrast, distantly related species, like maples and pines, enhance it significantly.

Additionally, a surge in species diversity can expand the community's genetic diversity. However, it might narrow the genetic range within individual species, primarily if heightened competition drives extreme specialization in species. Such competition can limit the genetic variety within each species.

Species Diversity

Biodiversity research predominantly centers on species. This focus isn't because species diversity holds greater importance but because species are more straightforward to study. Identifying species in their natural habitat is often simple, while gauging genetic diversity demands extensive lab work and resources. Evaluating ecosystem diversity requires long-term, intricate measurements.

Moreover, species offer a clear conceptual framework, having been the foundation for many evolutionary and ecological studies integral to understanding biodiversity.

Each species represents a unique facet of diversity and plays a specific role within its ecosystem. The introduction or displacement of a species can affect the entire system. Initiating conservation efforts occurs when experts identify a species as being at risk. A change in an ecosystem's species count provides a clear and understandable indicator of the ecosystem's health.

Ecosystem Diversity

Ecosystem-level theory focuses on species distribution, community patterns, and the roles and interactions of critical species. The term "ecosystem" encompasses levels beyond individual species, including associations, communities, and ecosystems.

While some researchers label these distinctions differently or break them into sub-levels like community and ecosystem, this overview combines them. Due to the intricate interplay of species and their surroundings, this remains the most challenging level to comprehend among the three discussed.

A significant challenge in studying communities is their often blurred transitions. For instance, while a lake might have a clear boundary with the surrounding deciduous forest, that same forest might transition more subtly into grasslands or coniferous woods. This phenomenon of indistinct boundaries is termed "open communities." Their nebulous nature complicates the study and even the definition of ecosystems.

While some scientists view communities as mere aggregates of their species and processes, many argue that communities possess unique attributes not derived from individual species. These distinct characteristics can include food web tiers, the species within those tiers, guilds (functionally similar species within a community), and other interspecies relationships.

Understanding the three levels of biodiversity is just the beginning. To grasp the full scope of our planet's rich biological tapestry, scientists employ specific methods and tools. Let's discuss how experts measure this vast array of life and assess the health of our ecosystems.

HOW SCIENTISTS MEASURE BIODIVERSITY

Scientists employ various methods and tools to measure biodiversity effectively. Understanding these techniques is crucial for assessing the richness of life on our planet and making informed conservation decisions. In this section, we'll explore how experts actively measure biodiversity across different levels and ecosystems.

Alpha Diversity

Alpha diversity refers to the combination within a distinct area or ecosystem, often a localized habitat. It captures the number of species and their comparative quantity in that specific site. In essence, alpha diversity provides a snapshot of the biodiversity richness and evenness at a single location or community.

When researchers study a forest patch or a pond, for example, they examine its alpha diversity to understand the variety and balance of life within that defined space.

Beta Diversity

Beta diversity is the divergence in species composition between various habitats or ecosystems within a more extensive area. It captures the turnover of species between two locations. For instance, if two forests have different sets of species due to variations in altitude, moisture, or other environmental factors, the difference in their species makeup represents beta diversity.

Understanding beta diversity helps scientists identify the factors that drive species distribution and informs conservation strategies by highlighting areas of unique species combinations.

Gamma Diversity

Gamma diversity refers to the total variety of species within a larger region or landscape, encompassing multiple ecosystems or habitats. It captures the combined biodiversity found across a vast geographical area, considering both the species unique to specific habitats and those shared among them. Gamma diversity offers a holistic picture of biodiversity on a larger scale.

How to Get Raw Data and Measure Species Richness

To understand biodiversity, we first conduct thorough surveys, identifying and counting species at specific sites. This raw data is like a chaotic book; its value emerges only after organizing and analyzing it. Consequently, we employ data visualization and statistical tools to decode this biodiversity narrative.

Understanding Species Richness

Species richness represents the count of distinct species in a selection. For instance, in a garden with one rose and one hundred tulips, both contribute equally to the richness, even if their numbers differ. It's akin to tallying distinct book titles in a bookstore without considering the quantity of each title. While richness hints at variety, it doesn't capture the entire essence of biodiversity.

The Rarefaction Curve: Gauging Diversity

Rarefaction curves, graphing species against samples, guide our understanding of species discovery rates. A steeper curve indicates that there are still more species to identify. Think of it like diving into a novel with many unfolding chapters. A flattening curve signals that we've uncovered most species in that area.

For example, in an aquatic survey, if adding more water samples doesn't reveal new fish species, we're likely close to understanding its full diversity.

Rank-Abundance Curve: Visualizing Species Distribution

The rank-abundance curve, or Whittaker plot, offers insights into species richness patterns. In a forest, a steep drop in the curve signifies dominance by a few species, while a gentle slope indicates an even distribution of species.

Relative Species Abundance: Gauging Species Popularity

This metric reveals the frequency of a species compared to others in a location or community. Take a meadow as an example. Observing twenty sunflowers and eighty daisies indicates that daisies are more prevalent in that meadow.

Fisher's Logarithmic Series Model: Mapping Abundance Relationships

Fisher's model mathematically illustrates the connection between species count and individual count within those species. This model refines our comprehension of species abundance. For example, in a tropical forest, this model might help predict the likely number of bird species based on the count of individual birds sighted.

The Downside of Quantitative Measures of Biodiversity

Counting species isn't as straightforward as it appears. Worldwide species estimates vary from 3 million to 100 million, but recent assessments suggest around 8.7 million (Ruiz, 2020). Yet many of these remain unidentified. When attempting to quantify species within a segment of an ecosystem, it's nearly impossible to account for every one due to the vast number present.

Moreover, distinguishing between species isn't always black and white. "Cryptic species" might closely resemble known species but possess distinct genetic differences, classifying them as separate entities.

Thanks to DNA sequencing advancements, we can now detect these species more efficiently. However, this has revealed another dimension of biodiversity: genetic divergence within a single species. Such variations increase a species' resilience against threats like climate change.

Additionally, a mere count of species doesn't reflect their ecological significance. Some "keystone species" profoundly influence ecosystem dynamics. For instance, reintroducing wolves to Yellowstone Park reshaped animal behavior and plant distribution, created niches for mammals like beavers, and even impacted the land's physical layout.

The Imperative of Holistic Biodiversity Conservation

Biodiversity's significance isn't just about the sheer number of species. Imagine a forest where specific species are endemic, butterflies on either riverbank possess unique genetic variants, or the entire forest's existence hinges on a single tree species. Which would you prioritize?

A comprehensive approach to assessing biodiversity value must recognize the intricate web of species interactions, as these often produce the ecosystem benefits we rely on. Protecting one species means safeguarding countless others, indirectly securing our future. In championing biodiversity, we ensure our well-being.

KEY TAKEAWAYS

- Biodiversity is vital for healthy ecosystems and supplies clean air, water, and food.
- Biodiversity encompasses all life forms on Earth, with millions of species, including insects, remaining unidentified.
- Biodiversity is crucial for practical benefits like resources, climate stabilization, and pest regulation, as well as its intrinsic cultural and spiritual value.
- Species richness calculates the number of distinctive species in an area, with different ecosystems having varying levels of diversity.
- Threats to biodiversity include invasive species, habitat loss, overexploitation, and climate change.

- Genetics, species, and ecosystem diversities are the three echelons of biodiversity, each playing a unique role in maintaining ecological balance.
- Scientists measure biodiversity through alpha, beta, and gamma diversity and use various tools like rarefaction curves and rank-abundance curves.
- Quantifying biodiversity is challenging due to the vast number of species and genetic variations within species.
- Holistic biodiversity conservation is essential to protecting ecosystems and ensuring our well-being.

Biodiversity is the bedrock of healthy ecosystems, offering many benefits and intrinsic value. Understanding its levels and measuring it is vital for informed conservation efforts. However, current practices globally are contributing to a loss of biodiversity. Let's discuss these practices further in the next chapter.

4

LOSING BIODIVERSITY—IS HOPE LOST?

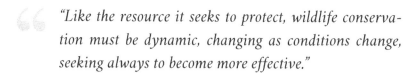 *"Like the resource it seeks to protect, wildlife conservation must be dynamic, changing as conditions change, seeking always to become more effective."*

— *RACHEL CARSON*

Rachel Carson's quote emphasizes that wildlife conservation should adapt and evolve to remain effective, like the ecosystems it aims to preserve. This philosophy underscores the need for proactive measures to address biodiversity loss in the U.S.

LOSS OF BIODIVERSITY IN THE UNITED STATES

NatureServe's recent analysis addresses five critical questions about biodiversity and conservation. The report reveals alarming statistics: 34 percent of plant and 40 percent of animal species are at risk of extinction, while 41 percent of ecosystems face potential collapse (*Biodiversity in Focus: United States Edition*, 2023).

This extensive assessment emphasizes the severity of the situation in U.S. ecosystems, with 51 percent of grasslands, 40 percent of forests, and wetlands at severe risk of collapsing across their entire range. Grassland loss, often underestimated, is a significant crisis, impacting iconic species and pollinators. Freshwater species and insects, including bees, face substantial threats (*Biodiversity in Focus: United States Edition*, 2023).

Threats to Biodiversity

The ongoing biodiversity loss in the United States results from a complex web of factors. Wetland destruction, waterway disruption through damming, invasive species, exotic wildlife diseases, and the overarching influence of climate change all contribute to this crisis. However, the primary drivers of species decline are habitat loss and degradation, which stem from the expansion of human dwellings.

Adding to these challenges are weak environmental laws, inadequate enforcement, and insufficient funding for conservation efforts. It's surprising that, on average, it requires twelve years, and in some instances, up to forty years, for the U.S. Endangered Species Act (ESA) to list species as endangered or threatened officially. Furthermore, only 5 percent of listed plants and animals receive adequate funding for conservation, with most resources allocated to a few high-profile species (Tolme, 2017).

The U.S. Fish and Wildlife Service (FWS), responsible for ESA listings, faces chronic underfunding and opposition from certain members of Congress seeking to restrict listings. The problem worsens due to the absence of specific funding channels allocated for animals categorized as "nongame."

1. **Freshwater fish:** Dam construction and river development threaten species like the pallid sturgeon and native trout in freshwater ecosystems. Disturbingly, 40 percent of North America's freshwater fish species are imperiled or extinct (Tolme, 2017).
2. **Freshwater mussels:** These mussels, including the rare golden riffleshell mussels, face extinction due to water pollution, sedimentation, and river alterations.
3. **Bumblebees:** Once abundant, they suffer from habitat loss, climate change, neonicotinoid pesticides, and disease.
4. **Butterflies:** Several butterfly species have gone extinct since 1950, with many more listed under the ESA.
5. **Amphibians:** Amphibians, including hellbender salamanders, are declining due to water quality degradation, habitat loss, disease, and nonnative species.

While there are success stories like the Sierra Nevada yellow-legged frog's resurgence, the overall situation demands urgent conservation efforts to protect imperiled species and preserve ecosystem balance.

United States Areas Most at Risk of Biodiversity Loss

Despite the severe repercussions of biodiversity loss, gathering information about which species are in distress and where they are facing challenges can be a complex task. Traditional maps typically concentrate on the broad geographical range of species, primarily on vertebrate animals.

However, a recent study in Ecological Applications delves deeper into the potentially appropriate habitats for various species across the entire United States, from the Santa Cruz Island Cypress to the Twisted Dwarf Crayfish to Cockerell's Bumblebee (Hamilton et al., 2022).

The study's findings are concerning. In the lower forty-eight states, there are nearly 300 vulnerable plant and animal species that exist entirely outside currently protected wildlife areas. These protected regions comprise just 13 percent of the continental United States, equivalent to around 316 million acres (Hamilton et al., 2022).

This discovery emphasizes that the United States is home to globally significant biodiversity beyond the well-known rainforests and coral reefs. The Biodiversity Importance Map underscores key regions essential for averting species extinction across the country.

The map highlights that the areas facing the highest risk for imperiled species are situated along the California coast and in the Southeastern region. The Southeastern part is home to a significant concentration of freshwater invertebrates under threat, with this area also hosting two vulnerable mussel species exclusive to Florida's Escambia River. At the same time, imperiled pollinators tend to focus along the Rust Belt and California's coast.

Moreover, among more than 800 species studied on national lands, approximately 85 percent lack protection under the Endangered Species Act. Of these, 326 species primarily inhabit federal multiple-use lands. About 66 percent of areas deemed crucial for biodiversity conservation lack protection, with most of these areas on private land (Hamilton et al., 2022).

Surprisingly, the research reveals that nearly 90 percent of Americans live within 30 miles of a highly significant zone for biodiversity preservation, underscoring the proximity of these hotspots to the population (Hamilton et al., 2022).

Is biodiversity loss reversible? This question becomes imperative when considering the urgent need to address the challenges outlined in the study. Exploring potential solutions and actions is crucial in the face of the alarming biodiversity loss revealed in the United States.

IS IT POSSIBLE TO REVERSE THIS LOSS?

Earth's biodiversity is under grave threat, with over a million species facing extinction, according to reports from the IPBES and the UN Convention to Combat Desertification. Human activities have transformed 70 percent of Earth's land, degrading up to 40 percent, while 87 percent of marine areas have been affected (*Explainer: Can the World 'Halt and Reverse' Biodiversity Loss by 2030?*, 2023).

A WWF report disclosed a shocking 68 percent average decline in populations of fish, reptiles, amphibians, birds, and mammals between 1970 and 2016, with a devastating 94 percent drop in tropical, central, and South America. This biodiversity crisis jeopardizes human well-being, risking $44 trillion and increasing the vulnerability of millions to floods and hurricanes while causing 430,000 annual deaths due to pollinator loss (*Explainer: Can the World 'Halt and Reverse' Biodiversity Loss by 2030,* 2023).

Efforts to counteract this trend through the Aichi targets faltered, prompting a call for a clear goal akin to climate change targets. In 2020, leaders from 94 countries pledged to reverse biodiversity loss by 2030, with 145 countries reaffirming commitments at COP26 in 2021. COP15 in 2022 included the mission to stop and flip biodiversity loss by 2030 in the Global Biodiversity Framework, signaling a renewed global commitment (*Explainer: Can the World 'Halt and Reverse' Biodiversity Loss by 2030,* 2023).

Is the 2030 Target Realistic?

Scientists concur that the goal of halting and reversing biodiversity loss by the end of this decade is a formidable challenge. The complexity of biodiversity, encompassing genes to ecosystems, makes it hard to measure and control. Unlike carbon, we can't replace biodiversity or make up for its loss in other places.

The response to actions to halt and reverse biodiversity loss varies among species and ecosystems. While some ecosystems recover within several years, others take half a century. Climate change exacerbates losses in systems like coral reefs, making the 2030 target doubtful. However, despite these challenges, scientists emphasize the necessity of aiming for this ambitious goal due to the severe consequences of further biodiversity loss.

Success will depend primarily on social, political, and financial responses by countries akin to climate change efforts. The Global Biodiversity Framework (GBF) includes targets addressing key drivers of biodiversity loss, such as harmful subsidies and pollution.

Conservation efforts within and outside protected areas are vital, with implementation and financing crucial factors. We must also tackle equity problems rooted in past resource consumption patterns and colonialism, as they play a role in the current biodiversity crisis.

Six Actions to Reduce Biodiversity Loss

A leading scientific team has outlined six critical actions to reverse terrestrial biodiversity loss due to land use change. Their study, published in Nature, suggests that by 2050, it's possible to halt and reverse this loss through an ambitious, integrated approach. This strategy combines conservation efforts, changes in food systems, and broader sustainability initiatives, including addressing climate change:

1. Achieving sustainable increases in crop yields.
2. Promoting increased agricultural trade with reduced trade barriers.

3. Reducing agricultural waste from production to consumption by 50 percent.

4. Cutting the human diet's portion of animal calories by 50 percent.

5. Expanding Protected Areas to cover 40 percent of terrestrial areas, focusing on critical biodiversity sites with improved management.

6. Increasing rehabilitation efforts, covering approximately 8 percent of land areas by 2050, and enforcing landscape-level protection planning that balances preservation and production goals across all controlled lands (*Strategy for Halting and Reversing Biodiversity Loss Revealed*, 2020).

These actions, if implemented comprehensively, offer a pathway to bend the arc of terrestrial biodiversity loss, offering hope for a more sustainable and biodiverse future.

Global Cooperation for Nature Conservation

Earth Hour 2022 witnessed the global community uniting in a resounding message of solidarity for the well-being of people and the planet. The call echoed the imperative of building a future where we coexist harmoniously with nature, one another, and our shared home.

To combat the alarming and accelerating decline of wildlife and natural habitats, WWF and its partners emphasize the urgent need for action within this decade. The goal is to establish a world inherently pro-nature by 2030, boasting more biodiversity than it does today.

Recent international deliberations sought to formulate a new United Nations strategy for restoring nature, potentially setting a course to counteract nature's deterioration.

Global Collaboration: A Prerequisite for Success

In the interconnected fabric of our planet, the issue of nature loss, much like climate change, knows no boundaries. Consequently, it necessitates a collective response, with countries uniting around a clear, unified pathway. Deforestation in the Amazon, for instance, transcends regional implications, as global demand for Amazonian products and climate change effects interweave. The recent UN biodiversity discussions indicate increasing accord towards the shared goal of flipping biodiversity loss by 2030, much akin to the 1.5 °C objective in the fight against climate change (*Four Ways to Reverse Nature Loss by 2030 for People and Planet*, 2022).

Financial Commitment: A Critical Pillar

The success of a global nature restoration plan hinges on robust financial support. With adequate funding, ambitions to reverse nature loss will remain strong. Disagreements persist among nations regarding the financing of biodiversity protection and the necessary transformations within financial systems to align with nature's interests. Developing countries advocate for increased funding for biodiversity efforts, but consensus on financing a new nature plan remains elusive. To enact real, on-the-ground change, enhanced financial commitments supported by comprehensive oversight are indispensable.

Inclusivity and Recognizing Indigenous Stewardship

Nature loss affects lives, jeopardizing poverty alleviation, social equity, and gender equality efforts. Inclusivity is of paramount concern, ensuring that every voice is heard, including histori-cally marginalized groups like women and young people. Moreover, local communities and Indigenous people are pivotal in protecting nature. As custodians of many remaining natural spaces, their rights must be respected and secured.

Leadership: A Call to Action

The collective voice of concerned individuals has compelled over ninety world leaders to commit to reversing biodiversity loss this decade. However, political leadership at recent biodi-versity negotiations fell short. We need to enhance leadership efforts to tackle both the challenges of climate change and biodiversity loss. This necessitates a robust focus on securing an ambitious pro-nature plan at COP15, with the essential elements of driving immediate action while bolstering climate initiatives. Together, we can ensure a world that is fair, nature-positive, and carbon-neutral.

As we explore the critical role of addressing biodiversity loss and climate change, the focus now shifts to agriculture. Agri-culture stands at the crossroads, pivotal in driving biodiversity loss and offering solutions to global crises.

AGRICULTURE: PRIMARY DRIVER OF BIODIVERSITY LOSS OR SOLUTION TO THE GLOBAL CRISIS?

The Chatham House report, with support from UNEP and Compassion in World Farming, highlights three crucial actions for transforming our food system to combat biodiversity loss. It emphasizes an urgent need, as the current international food system is the primary driver of biodiversity decline, threatening 86 percent of species at risk of extinction, totaling 24,000 (*Our Global Food System Is the Primary Driver of Biodiversity Loss,* 2021).

This alarming rate of species loss surpasses historical averages. In recent decades, focusing on "cheaper food" has led to increased use of inputs like fertilizers and pesticides, creating a harmful cycle. Moreover, the global food system's significant role in climate change, contributing to 30 percent of human-produced emissions, adds urgency to reform efforts (*Our Global Food System Is the Primary Driver of Biodiversity Loss,* 2021).

What Is Extensification?

Agriculture, whether involving crops or livestock, demands land, mainly prime farmland with fertile soil and water access. Unfortunately, this often leads to the conversion of these areas —which frequently host diverse ecosystems like prairies and forests—into farmland, resulting in the loss of natural biodiversity. This ongoing expansion of agriculture, known as *extensification*, threatens critical natural areas.

In the United States, for instance, grassland ecosystems like the tallgrass prairie, once teeming with diverse flora and fauna, were sustained by Indigenous practices like controlled fires. However, as settlers displaced native communities, these grasslands dwindled to 1 percent of their original expanse over a century and a half.

What Is Monocropping?

Industrial agriculture's heavy reliance on chemicals extends its impact beyond habitat destruction. *Monocropping*, a common practice, involves cultivating vast areas with a single crop, enabled by innovations like steel plows, hybrid seeds, GMOs, chemical fertilizers, and pesticides. While it boosts productivity, it turns fields into biodiversity deserts, requiring intensive chemical use that diminishes wild species on and around farms.

Pesticides and herbicides, meant to combat crop pests, inadvertently harm plants and animals beyond farm boundaries. Herbicide overuse and soil disturbance in intensive agriculture reduce plant diversity. Glyphosate, a widely used herbicide in the U.S., has significantly decreased wild plant diversity, affecting beneficial insects like monarch butterflies.

Insecticides, such as neonicotinoids, directly harm species like bees, impairing pollination. Some insecticides also threaten birds, amphibians, and fish. Agricultural pollution remains a primary threat to many global species, highlighting the need for sustainable farming practices.

How Industrial Agriculture Affects Soil Quality

Industrial agriculture also has detrimental effects on soil biodiversity. When farmers plow soil, it disrupts the habitats of insect and invertebrate communities, preventing them from efficiently decomposing dead plants into the stable organic carbon that enriches soils. Chemical use further harms the microorganisms crucial to this process, resulting in fewer beneficial bacteria and fungi species in soils treated with chemical fertilizers and pesticides.

Consequently, these soils become less diverse and less suitable for crop growth. Additionally, these changes contribute to climate change, as soil worldwide stores over 1.6 trillion tons of carbon dioxide (*Biodiversity and Agriculture*, 2021). However, highly disturbed soils with low biodiversity release carbon into waterways and the atmosphere at an accelerated rate. Sustainable soil management practices are essential to mitigate these negative impacts.

What Is Eutrophication?

Chemical use in agriculture can have far-reaching consequences for ecosystems beyond the farm. Nitrogen fertilizers, vital for plant growth, often run off into waterways, triggering harmful algae blooms that block sunlight and deplete oxygen upon their decay. This process, called *eutrophication*, occurs in both freshwater and saltwater environments. Excessive feces from factory farmsteads, rich in similar nutrients, also help eutrophication.

A well-known instance is the massive 6,000-square-mile dead site in the Gulf of Mexico, resulting from Midwest farm fertilizer runoff into the Mississippi River. Eutrophication reduces habitat availability, forces competition among species, and leads to biodiversity loss, necessitating efforts to mitigate these effects and maintain healthy ecosystems.

How Industrial Agriculture Affects Climate Change

Globally, industrial agriculture poses a significant threat to biodiversity as it contributes significantly to climate change. Agricultural emissions, primarily from chemical fertilizers and factory farming, account for over 20 percent of annual greenhouse gas emissions. Climate change is one of the most critical perils to biodiversity, affecting even distant, barely touched regions (*Biodiversity and Agriculture*, 2021).

Rising temperatures have already affected the reproductive patterns of migratory birds and other wildlife, while extreme weather events can dramatically alter plant and soil communities. This warming climate puts adaptable invasive species in a favorable position to outcompete specialized plants, animals, and microorganisms.

Scientists predict climate-induced biodiversity loss could become one of the most extensive mass extinctions in Earth's history. Mitigating these effects is paramount for preserving our planet's diverse ecosystems.

How Industrial Agriculture Affects Biodiversity

While thousands of edible plant species exist on Earth, the U.N.'s Food and Agriculture Organization (FAO) states that 75 percent of our food supply originates from twelve commonly cultivated plants and animals (*Biodiversity and Agriculture*, 2021). These selections, chosen for their consistency, have caused the displacement and extinction of many other grains, fruits, vegetables, and livestock breeds.

The loss of biodiversity in livestock and domesticated produce reduces the gene pool necessary for attributes like illness resistance, rendering our food supply vulnerable to diseases and climate change. Conserving undomesticated relatives of crop plants is crucial, as they harbor valuable imperiled genes.

Safeguarding crop and livestock diversity is also globally significant in terms of culture and diet. Genetic erosion is evident in the decline of agricultural biodiversity, accelerated by commercial breeding, hybrid seeds, and genetic modification. A few seed companies limiting choices have exacerbated this issue, leading to chemical-dependent monocultures dominated by modern crop varieties.

How Biodiversity Loss Affects Food Supply and Cultural Identity

Monocultures, chosen for farming consistency, threaten food security. The Gros Michel banana's near-extinction due to Panama Disease highlights this vulnerability, with the Cavendish banana now at risk. Other crops like wheat and apples face similar dangers, emphasizing the importance of preserving rare types.

Low-biodiversity farming worsens climate change and affects crop adaptability. Cultural identity and diverse cuisines rely on unique crops and livestock. Replacing local varieties with commercially bred ones compromises food sovereignty, undermines small farmers, and contributes to biodiversity loss.

How Biodiversity Promotes Sustainable Agriculture

Adopting agroecology, a farming approach that utilizes biodiversity to create sustainable agricultural ecosystems, offers a promising shift away from industrial farming. Agroecology draws from both traditional knowledge and modern research to maximize the benefits of nature in food production. Indigenous practices have long exemplified agroecological principles, maintaining complex systems in harmony with the environment.

Preserving these traditions can enhance global agricultural sustainability. Remarkably, 80 percent of the world's biodiversity resides on lands managed by Indigenous communities, highlighting agroecology's potential. Techniques like intercropping and agroforestry break monocultures, benefiting crops and wildlife while reducing environmental impact.

Livestock plays a crucial role in agroecosystems, enhancing soil fertility and biodiversity. Diverse livestock breeds adapt to various environments and contribute to a varied agroecosystem. Biodiverse agroecosystems create habitats for wild organisms, promoting natural pest control and pollination. By adopting agroecology, agriculture can prioritize sustainability, biodiversity, and traditional knowledge in food production.

The Focus of New Food Reform

The new Chatham House report emphasizes the urgency of reforming our food systems and highlights three interconnected actions:

1. Shifting global dietary patterns towards more plant-based diets is crucial. This change is necessary because animal husbandry disproportionately impacts the environment, land use, and biodiversity. Transitioning to plant-heavy diets, coupled with reducing food waste, will lower environmental pressure, improve global population health, and mitigate pandemic risks.
2. Increasing the protection and preservation of land for nature is essential. The most significant benefits for biodiversity arise from preserving or restoring entire ecosystems. It is critical to stop converting land for agriculture. Dietary shifts are crucial to conserving native ecosystems and rehabilitating degraded ones.
3. Adopting nature-friendly, biodiversity-supporting farming practices is vital. This involves reducing input use and replacing monoculture farming with polyculture methods.

Dietary changes are a prerequisite for enabling land restoration and promoting nature-friendly farming practices without further encroachment on natural habitats. Dietary change creates more opportunities for implementing the second and third actions.

KEY TAKEAWAYS

- Biodiversity loss is a critical issue with alarming statistics: 34 percent of plant species and 40 percent of animal species face extinction, and 41 percent of ecosystems are at risk of collapse in the United States.
- Primary drivers of biodiversity decline include habitat loss, climate change, weak environmental laws, and insufficient funding for conservation efforts.
- Weaknesses in the U.S. Endangered Species Act and funding allocation hinder species protection.
- Imperiled species such as freshwater fish, mussels, bumblebees, butterflies, and amphibians face severe threats.
- The U.S. is home to globally significant biodiversity, but many species lack protection.
- Reversing biodiversity loss by 2030 is challenging but essential, with global efforts and leadership required.
- Six critical actions can help reverse terrestrial biodiversity loss, including sustainable farming practices.
- Industrial agriculture is a significant driver of biodiversity loss, affecting soil, waterways, climate, and food security.

- Agroecology, drawing from traditional knowledge, promotes sustainable agriculture and biodiversity conservation.
- Shifting toward plant-based diets, protecting land for nature, and adopting nature-friendly farming practices are essential steps to combat biodiversity loss.

Addressing biodiversity loss is urgent and requires concerted global efforts, changes in food systems, and sustainability initiatives.

With a thorough knowledge of the crucial issues surrounding biodiversity loss and the essential actions required to combat it, let's explore the complexities and controversies inherent in wildlife management.

MAKE A DIFFERENCE WITH YOUR REVIEW

Unlock the Power of Generosity in Conservation

The Native American proverb, "We do not inherit the Earth from our ancestors; we borrow it from our children," encapsulates our duty to the planet and its wildlife. It's a call to action, urging us to preserve the natural world for future generations. Like you, many are seeking guidance on contributing to wildlife conservation and biodiversity, often feeling overwhelmed by the complexity of the subject.

Would you be willing to help guide these aspiring conservationists by sharing your thoughts on "Wildlife Conservation Decoded"?

Your review could be a beacon of hope and inspiration. It's not about recognition; it's about making a difference in someone's life and the world. Your words could encourage others to take action, to learn, and to make a positive impact on our environment.

GoldenPedal Publishing is committed to making wildlife conservation and biodiversity understandable and accessible to everyone with the publication of this book. Our mission is to spread knowledge and ignite passion for the environment. But we can't do this alone; we need your help to reach as many people as possible.

Think of your review as a small seed that could grow into a mighty tree of awareness and action. It's a simple, yet powerful act that can change lives and help preserve our planet's rich biodiversity. And it takes less than 60 seconds!

To leave your review, visit the following link or scan the QR code:

[https://www.amazon.com/review/review-your-purchases/?asin=B0CWYHG4R3]

If you believe in making a difference and helping others find their path in wildlife conservation, then you are part of our community, our tribe of change-makers.

Thank you for your support and for joining us on this important journey. Together, we can make a lasting impact on wildlife conservation and biodiversity.

With gratitude,

GoldenPedal Publishing

5

THE COMPLEXITIES AND CONTROVERSIES OF WILDLIFE MANAGEMENT

"The greatest threat to our planet is the belief that someone else will save it."

— *ROBERT SWAN*

Robert Swan's emphasis on personal responsibility in environmental care highlights the need for individual and collective action. Understanding wildlife management fundamentals is crucial to this approach, forming a critical aspect of our duty to protect and nurture our planet's rich ecosystems for future generations.

WILDLIFE MANAGEMENT: UNDERSTANDING THE BASICS

In conservation and ecological stewardship, mastering the fundamentals of wildlife management is the paramount issue.

This discipline plays a pivotal role in safeguarding biodiversity, promoting sustainable ecosystems, and fostering harmonious coexistence between humans and the natural world.

What Is Wildlife Management?

Wildlife management, crucial for balancing wild animal populations and their habitats, has evolved from focusing on game provision to encompassing broader ecological and societal benefits. It involves biologists and landowners collaborating to assess habitats and public expectations, leading to tailored strategies that can include habitat modification and guiding human interaction.

Objectives of Wildlife Management

Management is vital for conservation, using active strategies for wildlife and habitats. Wildlife managers focus on:

1. Boosting populations by enhancing habitat essentials.
2. Reducing populations like deer, who are harming crops, through controlled harvesting.
3. Stabilizing populations for sustained yield, ensuring continuous balance.

These efforts foster ecological balance and address human needs.

Why Manage Wildlife?

Landowners engaging in wildlife management reap both tangible and intangible rewards. Real benefits include revenue from leasing land for hunting and outdoor activities, along with ancillary services like guiding and hospitality. Intangibly, they enjoy wildlife observation, the satisfaction of habitat conservation, and a deepened connection with nature.

Carrying Capacity of Land

A crucial principle in wildlife management is that a land's ability to sustain animal life has limits. Central to many wildlife management strategies are two essential practices:

- Regulating population sizes to align with the land's carrying capacity.
- Managing the habitat to sustain or enhance this capacity.

Consider the following aspects regarding carrying capacity.

1. **Seasonal Variation:** The carrying capacity is typically higher in summer than in winter.
2. **Preparation for Extremes:** The capacity varies with environmental conditions, being higher in mild winters compared to harsh ones.
3. **Consequences of Overpopulation:** Exceeding carrying capacity can lead to habitat degradation, like overbrowsing, reducing the land's future capacity.

4. **Inter-Species Impact:** The presence of one species can affect the capacity available to another. For instance, elk overusing an area may make it less accessible for deer.
5. **Annual Fluctuations:** Factors such as snowfall, droughts, and availability of cover and food can cause yearly changes in carrying capacity.

Ideally, wildlife management aims for an optimum carrying capacity, striving to maintain animal populations at a level that the habitat can consistently support in good condition.

Habitat Management

Enhancing wildlife habitat requires informed decisions by landowners, moving beyond the notion that untouched areas are always best. Strategic vegetation management supports diverse wildlife, with game animals favoring younger vegetation, while species like red squirrels prefer mature forests.

This progression, termed "succession," describes how vegetation communities change, influenced by natural or human-induced events—post-disruptions, habitats evolve from grasses to mature forests or advanced prairies. For effective wildlife conservation, it's essential to anticipate and manage these stages, fostering varied habitats.

Diverse vegetation arrangements, known as "mosaics," cater to multifaceted habitat needs. Moreover, edges, where distinct vegetations converge, amplify habitat richness, especially with irregular boundaries.

Population Dynamics—How This Affects Wildlife Management

Wildlife populations often experience natural variations termed population cycles, varying in duration and intensity. Many species undergo cycles where populations surge until a limiting factor, such as food scarcity, triggers a sharp decline. The survivors face reduced competition, leading to healthier conditions and population resurgence. This cycle repeats over time.

A key objective of wildlife management is to regulate these cycles, primarily through hunting, to avoid population crashes. This approach prevents undue suffering, habitat degradation, and resource wastage. Some driving factors behind these cycles, like contagious diseases, are density dependent.

For instance, in dense coyote populations, the spread of diseases like mange becomes more prevalent. Other population fluctuations arise from lesser-understood factors, with some researchers pointing to phenomena like sunspots or random events.

How Population Management Differs from Individual Management

When managing wildlife, the focus should be on the population's well-being, even if individual animals might be adversely affected. Decisions should prioritize the larger population's health and stability.

For instance, while train-related deer fatalities are tragic, they don't threaten the overall deer population. Similarly, occasional hunting mishaps, such as accidentally shooting a pheasant hen, shouldn't negate the value of hunting as a management tool. Decisions must prioritize the broader population impact over individual outcomes.

Public Land Versus Private Land Management

Aldo Leopold, a central figure in wildlife management, emphasized the importance of private landowners to U.S. wildlife management in the 1930s (Knight, n.d.). While much of the wildlife interaction happens on public lands, especially in the Rocky Mountain West, the value of private land in conservation is undeniable. The challenge lies in actively involving landowners in conservation initiatives.

State-owned wildlife often depends on private lands for habitat, necessitating collaboration between landowners and wildlife agencies. The demand for guided hunts on private properties attests to their effective game management, often resulting in a higher percentage of trophy animals.

Public land managers, who cater to a diverse public, strive to maximize sustainable yields, often resulting in the predominant harvesting of younger animals. In contrast, private landowners can prioritize older animals, enhancing trophy quality, even if it limits hunting opportunities.

While public land management might face restrictions, private landowners can customize habitat enhancements, benefiting game populations. Yet, they must adhere to state and federal regulations encompassing timber harvest and endangered species protection.

In the Rocky Mountain region, while state agencies manage wildlife populations, federal entities focus on habitat, underscoring the significant role of private landowners in comprehensive wildlife management.

Recognizing the pivotal role of private landowners in wildlife management and exploring effective techniques and methods— these strategies enhance habitat, sustain populations, and ensure ecological balance, forming the cornerstone of responsible wildlife stewardship across diverse landscapes.

TECHNIQUES AND METHODS FOR WILDLIFE MANAGEMENT

Techniques and methods for wildlife management are vital for ensuring ecological harmony and sustainable use. Here are some of them:

Habitat and Community Manipulation

This approach involves managing specific species by influencing vital resources and their interactions with other species, including habitat alteration, predator-prey dynamics, competing species, and those significantly altering ecosystems. By regulating critical factors that determine species abundance, such as water, shelter, and predators, it's feasible to adjust their density and distribution.

The advancement in computing power has facilitated the application of spatially explicit models and Geographic Information Systems (GIS) techniques, allowing for detailed projections of the effects of various habitat modifications.

Mechanical

The most straightforward and effective strategy for mitigating wildlife damage involves using fencing for exclusion. This method boasts the benefits of being highly reliable and non-lethal. However, its implementation can be costly and requires substantial labor, including ongoing maintenance. Additionally, fencing extensive areas contributes to land fragmentation.

Behavioral

Modern wildlife deterrents target animal senses and thus come in acoustic, olfactory, or visual forms. Visual obstacles include not only traditional scarecrows but also predator silhouettes on large windows, preventing bird collisions. Acoustic deterrents encompass devices like gas cannons, which emit random explosions, and recordings of distress calls.

Ultrasonic deterrents, emitting sounds above 120 decibels and inaudible to most humans, can painfully affect animals with sensitive hearing, like canids.

Chemical compounds serve as sensory repellents. We can divide these into two categories:

1. Those that create a conditioned taste aversion by associating food with sickness.
2. Those that provide unpleasant sensory stimulation to the nervous system.

The former are known as aversive agents, while the latter are actual sensory repellents.

Immunization and Immunocontraception

These methods involve administering a vaccine to wildlife, either through direct capture and injection or indirectly via baited oral doses. A significant breakthrough in wildlife management over the past decade has been the control of rabies through oral immunization strategies. Immunocontraception is particularly appealing as a control method due to its potential for high species specificity, although it has limited success so far.

Biological

Biological control has primarily shown success in managing insect populations. One notable instance of its practical use in wildlife management is the introduction of the Myxoma virus to regulate the rabbit population in Australia, which is among the few successful cases. While it didn't completely eradicate the rabbits, this approach has successfully reduced their numbers to 20 percent of the original population size (Levin, 2013).

Direct Population Control

Direct population control involves either the reduction (through harvesting) or the increase (via reintroduction and translocation) of animal numbers. When dealing with game species, removal often occurs through regulated hunting guided by license quotas. This method is advantageous due to its species specificity, precise control over the number of animals removed, and minimal environmental impact.

On the other hand, reintroductions and translocations play a crucial role in bolstering existing populations and decreasing the risk of species extinction.

Wildlife Management Practices

1. **Monitoring Wildlife Populations:** Wildlife managers actively track the birth and death rates of species, along with the state of their habitats. This data is crucial for establishing hunting regulations and assessing the need for conservation strategies.
2. **Habitat Improvement:** To manage succession and its impact on wildlife, managers might clear or burn forests to stimulate new growth. This action helps increase the population of certain wildlife species.
3. **Hunting Regulations:** These are essential for safeguarding habitats and maintaining animal populations. Regulations set specific hunting times, bag limits, and legal hunting methods.

4. **Hunting as a Management Tool:** Effective hunting balances animal populations with their habitats and generates funds for wildlife management.

5. **Predator Control:** Managing predator populations is critical to helping threatened or endangered species establish stable numbers. This includes legal hunting and trapping of predators.

6. **Artificial Stocking:** Relocating animals from areas where they are plentiful to others with suitable habitats has proven effective in boosting game populations.

7. **Disease Control and Prevention:** Diseases like avian cholera significantly threaten wildlife, particularly in dense populations. Managers must act quickly to prevent disease spread, such as disposing of affected waterfowl.

8. **Management Funding:** Wildlife conservation is supported by the Pittman–Robertson Act (federal excise tax) and various state programs, providing essential financial resources.

Having explored diverse wildlife management practices, we will examine the controversial yet critical topic of culling. This technique, while effective for population control, raises significant ethical considerations. We'll now navigate this complex debate, assessing whether culling is a necessary aspect of wildlife stewardship or a practice needing reevaluation.

CULLING: AN EFFECTIVE WILDLIFE MANAGEMENT
TECHNIQUE OR INHUMANE AND OUTDATED
PRACTICE?

Culling, a method of wildlife population control, stands at the crossroads of ethical and ecological debates. This discussion explores its effectiveness in managing animal numbers versus the moral implications it raises, inviting a comprehensive understanding of whether culling remains a relevant practice in modern wildlife management or requires rethinking.

The Controversies Associated with Culling Animals

Conservation involves making critical decisions, often under pressing circumstances. It's reminiscent of playing an intricate game where clear outcomes are elusive, and the path to success is nebulous. Trade-offs, compromises, and challenging decisions are inevitable.

A prime example of such a trade-off is culling. Culling entails the targeted reduction of an animal population by selective killing. This method raises ethical questions as it tasks individuals with deciding the fate of animals, seemingly opposing the primary goal of conservation.

At first glance, the objective of conservation is to preserve all wildlife. Thus, eliminating any creature under the banner of protection seems counterintuitive.

Main Circumstances Where Culling Is Used

Culling plays a strategic role in wildlife management under specific scenarios. Understanding the main circumstances where it's employed offers clarity on its purpose and effectiveness.

Population Control

Culling is essential in conservation to manage biodiversity within finite spaces like national parks. When species exceed a park's carrying capacity, culling helps maintain ecological balance. Alternatives such as translocation, sterilization, and biocontrol are considered but often face challenges in feasibility and cost.

Invasive Species Management

Effective culling controls invasive species that harm native ecosystems. Despite the ethical concerns, especially when humans have introduced these species, culling remains a necessary, albeit complex, conservation strategy.

Disease Control in Wildlife

In the past, people have employed culling to prevent disease transmission in wildlife, and its effectiveness has shown variability. Cases like the UK's badger cull show the method's limitations in disease management, emphasizing the complexity of this approach in wildlife conservation.

Advantages of Culling

1. **Economic Benefits:** Properly conducted culling offers substantial financial gains. It bolsters tourism through hunting expeditions, like crocodile hunts in Australia and white-tail deer hunts in North America.
2. **Sustainable Populations:** Culling is crucial for ecosystem sustainability, preventing overpopulation, habitat degradation, and biodiversity loss. Examples include elephant and hippo culls in South Africa and bison in Yellowstone.
3. **Disease Control:** In effective management of animal diseases, culling prevents outbreaks like Anthrax and HPAI, as evidenced by Malaysia's response to the Nipah virus.
4. **Addressing Human Activity Conflicts:** Overpopulation of certain species, like emus in New Zealand and Canada geese in Colorado, can disrupt human activities, and are mitigated through culling.
5. **Enhancing Animal Health:** Culling maintains ecosystem health by removing sick or genetically inferior animals, thus strengthening overall genetic quality, as demonstrated in Texas deer management and livestock farming.

Disadvantages of Culling

1. **Unintended Harm to Biodiversity:** Culling often mistakenly targets non-threatening species, undermining biodiversity. South American initiatives against vampire bats mistakenly killed beneficial bats, while in New York and Australia, misdirected efforts impacted non-target mosquito and shark species, respectively.

2. **Unexpected Ecological Effects:** Initiatives like China's sparrow cull and Mauritius's flying fox cull led to ecological imbalances, causing famines and reduced crop yields due to disrupted natural pest control.

3. **Ethical Concerns:** Culling raises ethical issues due to inhumane practices, as seen in the poultry industry and Canadian seal hunts, necessitating more compassionate methods.

4. **Population Increase Paradox:** In Tasmania and Britain, culling feral cats and ferrets increased their population due to reduced competition and resource availability.

5. **Risk of Accelerating Extinction:** Culling can dangerously hasten the extinction of vulnerable species like elephants, sharks, and rhinos. Practices like shark drum lines and elephant culling counteract conservation efforts, emphasizing the need for alternative population control strategies.

Alternatives to Culling

The alternatives to culling mentioned include:

1. **Exclusion:** This involves creating physical barriers to prevent animals, like deer, from disrupting plant communities. An example is the use of fencing to protect specific areas from animal intrusion.
2. **Establishment of Mega-Parks:** Proposed by Professor Rudi van Aarde, this concept involves linking regions with growing animal populations to those with declining numbers to achieve stability across a larger area (van Aarde & Jackson, 2007). This is particularly relevant for elephant population management.
3. **Surgical Sterilization:** The Elephant Population Management Program suggests a surgical vasectomy program for bull elephants (van Wyk, 2016). This method aims to control overpopulation effectively and humanely while maintaining the animals' social hierarchy.
4. **Oral Vaccination Programs:** In Europe, the spread of rabies among foxes has been controlled by distributing baits containing an oral vaccine. This approach has significantly reduced rabies cases without resorting to culling.

These alternatives highlight the importance of humane, sustainable, and ecologically mindful methods for managing wildlife populations, moving away from the potentially harmful culling practices.

The War on Wolves in the United States

The grey wolf population in North America, once on the brink of extinction, rebounded to about 7,500 in the lower forty-eight states by 2020, thanks to the 1973 Endangered Species Act (Joosse, 2021). Recently, however, the species has faced new challenges.

With their removal from federal protection in 2021, state-managed hunts have significantly reduced their numbers. Wisconsin's aggressive hunting strategies, including a planned hunt with a 300-wolf quota, have sparked concerns among experts about detrimental impacts on the ecosystem and wolf population stability (Joosse, 2021).

This situation underscores the critical need for careful, sustainable wildlife management to ensure the continued recovery and health of gray wolves.

Disruption to Study of Yellowstone Park Packs

Intense wolf hunting in the northern Rocky Mountains, including parts of Yellowstone National Park, has resulted in over 500 wolves killed in Montana, Idaho, and Wyoming, raising concerns about the stability of wolf populations and ongoing ecosystem research (Morrel, 2022).

Changes in legal protection have shifted wolf management from federal to state levels, with some states aggressively reducing wolf numbers. This has affected wolf pack structures and complicated scientific studies in Yellowstone (Morrel, 2022). The contradiction in state policies has sparked legal challenges and calls for more balanced wildlife management practices.

WHERE NATURE AND CITIES COLLIDE: CAN WE LIVE HARMONIOUSLY WITH WILDLIFE?

Rapid global population growth has led to significant habitat loss for many animals. In response, wildlife conservation initiatives aim to foster coexistence between humans and animals. With strategic planning and community involvement, it's feasible for both to thrive alongside each other.

Can People and Wildlife Live Alongside Each Other?

In Gudalur, India, a tiger's fatal attacks on two individuals triggered intense public outcry and media sensationalism. The subsequent search and killing of the tiger, amid protests and clashes, highlighted critical conservation challenges (Thekaekara, 2018). This incident underlines the need for nuanced solutions in wildlife-human interactions and management.

Human-Wildlife Conflict

In India's dense population, the human-wildlife conflict is a nuanced challenge, with humans and animals competing for the same space and resources. This is particularly significant given India's substantial numbers of tigers and Asian elephants.

While cultural and religious practices have traditionally supported coexistence, the success of protected areas has ironically led to increased intolerance towards wildlife in shared spaces. Prompt action is essential in extreme cases, like tiger or leopard attacks, underscoring the need for better training for field staff.

Historically, there was significant tolerance towards wildlife in India, a sentiment that is waning today. Understanding and respecting the cohabitation of rural and forest communities with wildlife is vital, and urban conservationists must recognize these complexities before criticizing actions taken against dangerous wildlife.

The Human-Human Conflict

The human-human conflict, stemming from colonial-era control over India's forests, persists today, with forest inhabitants often feeling sidelined. Post-independence India upheld these dynamics, potentially for national cohesion, leading to challenges like those seen in the Nilgiris district. Here, locals and the forest department clash over allegations of outside agitation and departmental negligence.

Historical reports of forest department malfeasance, coupled with contentious land ownership laws like the 1949 Tamil Nadu Act, intensify these disputes (Thekaekara, 2018). The Nilgiris district, under threat from illegal activities, requires balanced state intervention. For wildlife conservation success, India needs a comprehensive approach that addresses forest community grievances.

The Situation in the United States

Determining the precise start of wildlife returning to American cities is challenging, yet Disney's 1942 *Bambi* marks a significant point. Post-World War II, changing attitudes and suburban expansion increased deer populations in urban areas. Legislation from the 1960s aimed at endangered species protection and reduced predator control further facilitated this urban wildlife resurgence.

Consequently, urban areas frequently encounter various animals, from smaller species like foxes and raccoons to larger mammals such as bobcats and bears. Alligators, aquatic mammals, and even fishers have notably returned to urban habitats. This resurgence prompts speculation about future wildlife, like coyotes, in urban settings.

Urban dwellers often respond with surprise or fear to wildlife encounters, due to misconceptions about animal habitats and dangers. However, most large animals pose less risk than smaller species. Current city responses to wildlife could be more efficient and highlight the need for better, science-based urban wildlife management strategies.

A modern strategy for managing urban wildlife should encompass four key components:

1. Research is vital for effective management, particularly since wildlife scientists have a limited understanding of urban ecosystems due to their focus on more untouched environments.

2. Educational initiatives are essential to correct misconceptions and build community support.
3. Upgrading infrastructure, such as implementing wildlife-proof garbage bins, installing street signs, and using bird-friendly window treatments, is necessary to minimize conflicts between humans and wildlife while safeguarding the animals.
4. Developing explicit policies and enhancing coordination among agencies dealing with urban wildlife is essential for comprehensive planning and handling of severe but occasional incidents.

These steps are critical to ensure harmonious coexistence between America's growing urban populations and the wildlife adapting to city life.

KEY TAKEAWAYS

- Wildlife management has evolved to focus on ecological and societal benefits, involving collaboration between biologists and landowners to tailor strategies.
- The carrying capacity of land is crucial, influenced by factors like seasonal variation, environmental conditions, overpopulation consequences, inter-species impact, and annual fluctuations.
- Habitat management involves informed decisions by landowners to enhance wildlife habitat through strategic vegetation management and fostering diverse habitats.

- Wildlife management techniques and methods encompass habitat and community manipulation, mechanical, behavioral, immunization, biological, and direct population control strategies.
- Culling is a controversial topic in wildlife management, with advantages such as economic benefits and disease control but disadvantages like unintended harm to biodiversity and ethical concerns.
- Coexistence between humans and wildlife is possible through strategic planning and community involvement, addressing human-wildlife conflicts.
- Urban areas encounter various wildlife species, requiring better science-based urban wildlife management strategies involving research, education, infrastructure upgrades, and policy development for harmonious coexistence.

As we learn about wildlife management, let's explore additional methods and strategies that play a crucial role in ensuring the well-being of animal populations and their habitats in the next chapter.

6

FURTHER WILDLIFE
MANAGEMENT METHODS

"When you realize the value of all life, you dwell less on what is past and concentrate on the preservation of the future."

— *DIAN FOSSEY*

D ian Fossey's words highlight that recognizing the importance of all living beings shifts our focus from past losses to proactive efforts in conserving and protecting life for future generations. Her perspective seamlessly leads to the concept of species reintroduction, a conservation measure that directly contributes to the preservation of biodiversity.

SPECIES REINTRODUCTION

Species reintroduction is a conservation strategy that re-establishes populations of animals in their native habitats from which they have been extirpated, aiming to revive ecosystems and sustain biodiversity through well-researched and managed releases.

What Are Species Reintroductions?

Species reintroduction involves placing animals back into regions where they once naturally lived but disappeared due to various factors, aiming to restore ecological balance and conserve biodiversity. These efforts are strategic and rooted in extensive scientific research to ensure their success and sustainability.

What Is Rewilding?

Conservation biology focuses on preserving ecosystems and reducing species extinction by enhancing biodiversity and preserving natural habitats. This field operates at various levels, such as safeguarding ospreys in Scotland and tracking species extinction globally through the IUCN Red List.

Rewilding, a branch of conservation biology, is gaining recognition as a potent strategy for ecological restoration and for repairing damage caused by human activities over the last few centuries. Rewilding was recently introduced and is subject to different interpretations. It is the scientific reasoning behind extensive wilderness restoration, emphasizing the role of large predators in maintaining ecosystem balance.

This concept stems from the idea that apex predators have a significant, cascading impact on other species in the food web, thereby stabilizing ecosystems. Nonetheless, some rewilding efforts focus on reintroducing various keystone species, not exclusively large predators, which can still profoundly influence their environment.

Case Study—Reintroducing the Tasmanian Devil to Australia

Amid the often grim environmental news, it's incredibly uplifting to learn of successful efforts to restore endangered species to their natural habitats. Areas once home to the European bison and Tasmanian devil have witnessed the active reintroduction of these species.

The term frequently used by the press, "release," marks a pivotal phase in the broader process known as species reintroduction. This process entails re-establishing a species in its former environment, carefully selecting healthy individuals, and determining their release site.

Insurance Population and Genetic Considerations

Maintaining an insurance population is a critical first step in species reintroduction, requiring answers to crucial questions regarding the appropriate habitat for reintroduction and the best source of individuals for breeding. In the case of the Tasmanian devil, this involved establishing an insurance population in 2006 after carefully monitoring their health and genetic diversity. These efforts are essential to ensure a healthy and genetically varied group of individuals that can survive and thrive post-release.

Selection of the Release Site

Choosing a release site for reintroduction requires matching the introduced species with established local populations to avoid genetic issues like outbreeding depression. Simulations predict reintroduced species' adaptations and ecosystem impacts, like Tasmanian devils controlling invasive species, but long-term post-release studies must confirm these outcomes.

Monitoring and Evaluation

Following the reintroduction of species like the European bison and Tasmanian devil, vigilant monitoring is essential to assess their survival and reproductive success, as well as to maintain genetic diversity. This ongoing surveillance informs and refines conservation strategies.

Since these species are reentering habitats, they've been absent for, in some cases, thousands of years, and verifying the current suitability of these environments is critical. Embracing a multi-disciplinary approach that marries conservation genetics with ecology is vital for ensuring the well-being of entire ecosystems. Celebrating these efforts necessitates acknowledging the complexity and interconnectedness of natural habitats and their inhabitants.

The Pros and Cons of Species Reintroduction

Exploring the pros and cons of species reintroduction unveils the delicate balance between reviving ecosystems and the challenges of re-establishing species within their former habitats, a process both crucial for biodiversity and fraught with complex ecological implications.

Pros of Species Reintroduction

- **Ecological Balance**

Reintroduced species can restore natural processes and dynamics in ecosystems that have been lost, often improving overall environmental health. Apex predators like wolves and lynx can regulate prey populations and foster biodiversity.

- **Biodiversity Enhancement**

Reintroductions often aim to increase the genetic diversity of small or isolated populations, contributing to the species' resilience. Various species, including pine martens, have been shown to benefit other wildlife and increase the overall biodiversity of their habitats.

- **Habitat Improvement**

Beaver activities create diverse habitats conducive to numerous species, supporting a complex and rich ecosystem. The modifications in the landscape, such as the creation of pools and wetlands by beavers, benefit species such as ducks, supporting hunters' interests.

- **Conservation Engagement**

Projects invite engagement from local communities and stakeholders, creating awareness and education about conservation. Shooters, poultry keepers, and farmers are given platforms to voice concerns and contribute to management plans, fostering collaborative conservation.

Cons of Species Reintroduction

- **Potential Conflicts**

Predatory species can pose risks to game birds, livestock, and the interests of various stakeholders, leading to resistance against reintroduction projects. Reintroduction can require an adjustment period for local populations and ecosystems, sometimes leading to conflicts.

- **Habitat Modification Risks**

Species like beavers alter their environments significantly, which can have unforeseen impacts on water management and land use. Tree felling and damming activities by beavers may conflict with human activities and land development plans.

- **Adaptation Challenges**

Reintroduced animals may face challenges adapting to current habitats that may have changed since they were last present. There is a risk that introduced individuals may need to integrate better with existing populations due to genetic or behavioral discrepancies.

- **Resource Intensiveness**

Reintroduction programs often require significant financial, human, and time resources for monitoring and management. Ongoing management efforts may be necessary to resolve conflicts and ensure peaceful coexistence between reintroduced species and local communities.

Species reintroduction is a complex conservation strategy with the potential for significant ecological benefits and challenges. Success often depends on thorough planning, community engagement, and continued management to balance the needs of wildlife with those of local stakeholders.

Rewilding Case Studies: United Kingdom versus United States

Rewilding efforts in the U.K. and the U.S. present contrasting case studies, offering insights into the diverse strategies and outcomes of ecosystem restoration and species conservation in different geographical and sociopolitical contexts.

Reintroduction of Beavers into Scotland

Over the last twenty-five years, rewilding projects have seen varied outcomes, with the reintroduction of the Eurasian beaver to Scotland standing out as a notable success. The Eurasian beaver, which was hunted to extinction in Great Britain for its fur and castoreum, has made a comeback, bolstering biodiversity as a keystone species.

Research endorsing their reintroduction followed IUCN guidelines, confirming historical records of their existence and addressing the reasons for their prior extinction.

Beavers have reshaped Scottish landscapes by creating new habitats through their natural activities like damming and foraging, benefiting a diverse range of species and vegetation. These natural engineers have also contributed to flood and drought management, providing cost-effective ecological services.

Economically, beavers have become a source of ecotourism revenue, drawing visitors and supporting local businesses, potentially adding over £2 million per year to the economy (Campbell et al., 2007). Their role as a flagship species has further promoted conservation awareness, fueling interest in environmental initiatives. This rewilding success story illustrates how such projects can offer significant environmental and economic benefits.

Reintroduction of Grey Wolves at Yellowstone National Park

The United States national parks serve as arenas for successful rewilding, exemplified by the reintroduction of gray wolves to Yellowstone. This initiative has restored ecological balance by altering elk behaviors and allowing aspen groves to flourish. The wolves have also regulated coyote populations, aiding in species diversification.

Beyond ecological restoration, the wolves have buffered climate change impacts and boosted local economies through ecotourism, with over $5 million generated from increased visitor interest in the restored wolf populations (Gray Wolves Increase Tourism in Yellowstone National Park, 2011).

This triumph in Yellowstone underscores the broader implications of managing predators as crucial agents in ecological networks. Beyond rewilding landscapes, managing predator species, such as wolves, plays a pivotal role in maintaining the health of ecosystems, influencing climate resilience, and even spurring economic growth through wildlife-based tourism.

MANAGING PREDATORS

In wildlife management, the effective management of predators plays a pivotal role in maintaining ecological balance and safeguarding vulnerable prey populations.

What Is Predation?

Predation involves capturing prey for sustenance, serving as a natural and vital process in ecosystems. Typically, predator and prey populations fluctuate naturally, with neither reaching excessively high nor low levels of concern for wildlife managers. However, there are instances where predation can pose a significant threat to wildlife populations.

Why Predator Management Is Necessary

Predator management is vital in livestock operations like sheep and goat farming to maintain profitability. With the increasing economic importance of wildlife, primarily through hunting leases, a key question arises: Should predators be controlled to protect wildlife populations?

To decide, evaluate predation's impact on local wildlife, considering factors beyond increasing numbers. Before starting a predator management agenda, ask:

- Is predation genuinely restricting local wildlife?
- Can we support a larger game population by controlling the number of predators in available habitats?
- Can surplus game from predator control be harvested to justify such measures?

Ecosystem Role of Predators

Conservation actions aimed at top predators are ecologically justified because they enhance biodiversity. Predators play a crucial role in shaping ecosystems, as illustrated by the consequences of sea otter overexploitation, which led to a sea urchin population surge and kelp bed destruction.

Managing predator populations is complex; reducing them to benefit prey can backfire, causing disease outbreaks. Predators often trigger trophic cascades, like Yellowstone's wolf recovery aiding aspen and willow resurgence, thus helping various species. Human activities, such as tourism displacing cougars in Zion National Park, can also trigger trophic cascades affecting vegetation.

Issues around Decisions to Manage Predators

Preserving top-level predators is crucial for natural processes in national parks, but conflicts with predators, including livestock predation, pet threats, and rare human encounters, are common. Expanding cougar and wolf populations in North

America present challenges in managing big game species, especially in Alaska and Canada.

Predator management methods and positive public perception are essential, even though some effective lethal techniques face opposition. Predators can threaten endangered species, necessitating control, and coexisting with predators requires adapting hunting practices to maintain prey populations. Effective predator management considers ecosystems, recognizing predators' ecological importance to minimize drastic measures.

Factors Affecting Predation

1. Predator populations can temporarily swell following a surge in their primary prey, such as coyotes with rabbits. Should the prey numbers drop rapidly, predators may switch to hunting alternative species.
2. Human activities, like road construction or land clearing, as well as natural events like drought, can force prey into confined spaces, increasing their vulnerability to predators.
3. Human developments, such as artificial feeding sites or water installations in dry regions, can inadvertently create prey hotspots, drawing in predators.
4. The age structure of predator populations may influence predation patterns, with some suggesting older coyotes may hunt more young deer.
5. Imbalanced sex ratios in deer, with the dominance of females, may lead to a drawn-out breeding season,

leaving bucks more susceptible to predation post-rut and extending the time fawns are at risk.

Understanding factors that affect predation is crucial when considering an Integrated Pest Management (IPM) approach. Various elements, such as prey population dynamics, human activities, and predator demographics, can impact predation patterns. By integrating these insights into an IPM strategy, one can effectively manage predator-prey interactions and minimize potential conflicts.

Integrated Pest Management Approach

Integrated Pest Management (IPM), a mainstay in agriculture, adapts well to managing predators. This approach acknowledges that predators can be both beneficial and destructive, depending on the context. Regular monitoring is crucial to assess predator and prey numbers and the extent of any damage caused by predators.

Economic thresholds guide decisions on when to implement control actions. Typically, managing predators requires a mix of lethal and nonlethal tactics.

How to Scout for Population Numbers and Interpret Signs

In a predator management program guided by Integrated Pest Management (IPM), the initial step is to identify the predator and prey species on your property and determine if an issue with predators exists. This process involves understanding local wildlife through aerial and whistle counts to monitor population trends and assess the impact of predators on game species.

Recognizing predator presence through tracks and scent stations and analyzing predator scat—containing prey wastes— provides valuable insights. Camera systems strategically placed can monitor game and predator activities, and examining evidence like hair in fences and investigating kill sites helps distinguish predation from other causes of wildlife loss. Careful examination of physical evidence and signs allows for the verification of predation and identification of the predator responsible.

Determining Control Methods

Developing an effective control strategy for managing predators is crucial, and it should take into consideration several key factors:

1. **Target Species:** Identify the specific predators you want to control.
2. **Scale of Control:** Determine the scope and extent of predator control required, whether it's a small localized area or a larger region.
3. **Season and Duration:** Consider the timing and duration of predator control activities, which may vary based on factors like breeding seasons.
4. **Lethal and Nonlethal Methods:** Decide whether fatal (resulting in the predator's death) or nonlethal methods

(disrupting their ability to cause harm) are more suitable for your objectives.

5. **Cost-Benefit Ratio:** Evaluate the cost-effectiveness of different control methods and their impact on your overall goals.

6. **Result Evaluation:** Plan how you will assess the outcome and effectiveness of your predator control program over time.

There are various methods available for predator control, categorized into lethal and nonlethal options:

Nonlethal Methods

1. **Habitat Enhancement:** Improve the prey species' habitat by enhancing nesting cover and other environmental factors.

2. **Fencing:** Use fences to protect against free-ranging dogs and other predators effectively.

3. **Cage Traps ("Live Traps"):** Capture animals alive without harming them, suitable for various species.

4. **Conditioned Taste Aversion:** An experimental method associates food taste with predator illness, potentially deterring them.

5. **Immunocontraception:** Another practical approach that aims to control predator populations through immunization.

Lethal Methods

1. **Foothold Traps:** Although not always lethal, these versatile traps capture various predator species. They are, however, widely considered to be inhumane causing the animal to suffer.
2. **Neck Snares:** Simple and effective, though not highly selective.
3. **Calling/Shooting:** Selective but time-consuming, involves calling predators and then shooting them.
4. **Aerial Gunning:** Highly effective in some situations but can be costly. It is typically used for specific predator species.

Select your control method based on your management objectives, whether optimizing game for hunting, bolstering game numbers, maintaining predator-prey balance, or reducing game populations. Be mindful of legal regulations at local, state, and federal levels.

Periodically assess your predator management program, considering external factors like environmental conditions and diseases that affect wildlife populations. Prioritize legality and ethics in implementing control methods, emphasizing the importance of meticulous planning and comprehensive consideration of all relevant factors for effective predator management.

Ethics of Predator Management

Wildlife managers, like many professionals, can benefit from adopting a code of ethics to guide their actions in predator management. While it's a personal choice to adhere to such a code, responsible wildlife managers should embrace ethical behavior to ensure their predator control practices are beyond reproach. Ethical predator management involves the following principles:

1. **Compliance with Laws and Regulations:** Strictly follow all laws, regulations, and predator control policies.
2. **Respect for People, Property, and Wildlife:** Maintain very high levels of regard for human beings, their possessions, and the welfare of wildlife.
3. **Conservation of Natural Resources:** Prioritize the preservation of natural resources and the environment in all predator management activities.
4. **Recognition of Ecological Value:** Acknowledge that predators play an essential role in ecosystems and contribute to ecological balance.
5. **Respect for Diverse Perspectives:** Respect differing viewpoints on predator management, recognizing that it can be a contentious issue.
6. **Target-Specific Control:** Accurately identify the species responsible for losses and focus control efforts exclusively on that species.

7. **Continuous Learning:** Continuously expand knowledge and skills related to predator management through education and experience.
8. **Humane and Selective Methods:** Choose control methods that are humane, selective, and effective in achieving management goals.
9. **Regular Monitoring:** Monitor traps and snares regularly to minimize unintended catches and reduce animal suffering.
10. **Humane Dispatch:** Humanely eliminate suffering by swiftly euthanizing animals caught in traps.
11. **Proper Carcass Disposal:** Dispose of animal carcasses properly, avoiding practices like hanging them on fences or in trees.

Recognize the influence of public perception on predator management and the development of relevant laws and regulations. Disseminate scientifically informed, research-based information to the public.

Practice a "good neighbor policy" by collaborating with neighboring landowners, discussing goals and methods, and supporting local predator management associations for more effective efforts.

Ethical predator management entails adhering to laws, respecting diverse viewpoints, prioritizing conservation, and using humane, selective approaches while fostering collaboration for shared objectives.

Understanding the influence of public perception on predator management guides us toward humane, ethical practices. Similarly, managing disease in wildlife populations requires collaborative, informed strategies to ensure ecological health, highlighting the need for shared knowledge and action in the transition to disease management principles.

MANAGING DISEASE

Managing disease in wildlife is a critical endeavor that demands proactive measures to safeguard both animal populations and ecosystems. Effective disease management is crucial for maintaining the health and balance of natural environments.

The Impact of Disease on Wildlife

Wildlife mortality from disease is escalating due to habitat loss, climate change, and increased contact with humans and domestic animals. Notable conditions include White-Nose Syndrome in bats, decimating populations across North America, and Chytridiomycosis in amphibians, causing declines globally.

Additionally, Chronic Wasting Disease in deer and elk poses a significant threat, with cases spreading through the United States and Canada. These diseases, exacerbated by environmental stresses, underscore the intricate balance between wildlife health and ecosystem stability.

The Importance of an Emergency Response

An effective emergency response to wildlife disease safeguards biodiversity and ecosystem health. Quick action can contain outbreaks, preventing widespread mortality that disrupts food webs and habitat function. It also mitigates the threat of diseases transferring to household creatures or humans. Proactive measures include surveillance, habitat management, and vaccination programs, ensuring resilient wildlife populations.

This responsiveness not only protects wild species but also upholds the integrity of natural systems that support human life and livelihoods, reflecting the interdependence of all species on Earth.

A Focus on Disease Prevention

Focusing on disease prevention in wildlife is essential; it maintains ecological balance and conserves species. Strategies like habitat preservation, species monitoring, and immunization campaigns preempt outbreaks, securing the health of ecosystems and the myriad forms of life, including human, that depend on them.

Why Attempt Management of Disease in Wildlife?

Managing disease in wildlife is imperative to preserve animal populations, as unchecked illnesses can lead to significant declines or extinctions. It also curbs potential transmission to humans, addressing zoonotic threats that can cause widespread health crises. Domestic animals, too, are at risk, with diseases from wildlife potentially impacting agriculture and livelihoods.

Public pressure often necessitates such management, reflecting growing concern over environmental health and animal welfare. Therefore, controlling disease in wildlife requires a complex approach, essential to safeguard the natural world and the interlinked interests of human and domestic animal populations.

Options for Disease Management in Wildlife

1. **Do nothing:** This hands-off approach accepts disease as a natural regulatory mechanism, though it can risk extensive biodiversity loss.
2. **Prevention of disease:** Proactive measures like habitat conservation and species vaccination mitigate disease emergence, promoting robust wildlife populations.
3. **Control of disease:** When prevention falls short, targeted actions such as culling, treatment, and population surveillance manage disease spread and impact.
4. **Eradication of disease:** The most ambitious option aims to eliminate a disease, often through extensive vaccination and stringent wildlife management protocols, securing ecosystem health.

Intervention in Host Populations—Vaccination Intervention

Pros

- Vaccination can significantly reduce disease prevalence in host populations, enhancing their survival and reducing the risk of outbreaks.
- It helps maintain biodiversity by protecting vulnerable species, contributing to overall ecosystem stability.

Cons

- Targeting incorrect strains or facing rapidly evolving pathogens can render vaccination efforts ineffective.
- It may inadvertently harm wildlife, disrupting natural immune responses or causing side effects.
- Implementing vaccination programs in wild populations is often logistically challenging and costly.

Manipulating Number, Density or Distribution of Host Animals

1. Dispersal is employed to manage host animal populations by relocating them to adjust distribution, using controlled releases to lessen densities in targeted areas or enhance colonization elsewhere.
2. Fencing effectively contains or redirects animal movement, establishing boundaries that control their spatial distribution, which is essential for disease management.

3. Removing diseased animals is crucial; it involves actively identifying and eliminating infected individuals from the population, thereby improving overall health and altering the distribution and density of the remaining healthy animals.

KEY TAKEAWAYS

- Species reintroduction involves placing animals back into their natural habitats to restore ecological balance and conserve biodiversity.
- Rewilding is a preservation technique that restores ecosystems and aids species conservation, often by reintroducing keystone species or large predators.
- Predator management is essential for maintaining ecological balance and safeguarding prey populations.
- Integrated Pest Management (IPM) involves monitoring, assessing, and selecting control methods for predators, considering economic thresholds.
- Managing disease in wildlife is critical to preserving biodiversity, preventing zoonotic transmission, and protecting domestic animals and human interests.
- Manipulating host animal numbers, density, or distribution involves dispersal, fencing, and removing diseased animals to manage disease spread and impact effectively.

As we discuss further wildlife conservation battles, it's crucial to recognize how rising temperatures and disrupted habitats accelerate species decline. You'll understand the impact of climate change on wildlife conservation next.

7

CLIMATE CHANGE: THE REAL IMPACT ON WILDLIFE CONSERVATION

"Until we consider animal life to be worthy of the consideration and reverence we bestow upon old books and pictures and historic monuments, there will always be the animal refugee living in a precarious life on the edge of extermination, dependent for existence on the charity of a few human beings."

— *GERALD DURRELL*

Gerald Durrell suggests that animals need to be valued as cultural treasures, implying their survival is now reliant on limited human goodwill.

Exploring climate change unearths its profound effects on wildlife. As habitats alter and temperatures shift, species face an existential threat, underscoring the urgency for comprehensive climate action.

UNEARTHING CLIMATE CHANGE: THE EXTENT OF IMPACT ON WILDLIFE

Rising temperatures have a widespread impact on wildlife, revealing how disrupted ecosystems and shifting climates threaten biodiversity and necessitate immediate conservation efforts.

HOW CLIMATE CHANGE THREATENS BIODIVERSITY

Currently, the Earth's temperature has increased by approximately 1.1 °C (2 °F) since the nineteenth century. Projections indicate that, by the century's end, we could see a global temperature increase of 2.7 °C (4.8 °F). Forecasting the precise consequences of these enduring temperature and weather pattern shifts on our planet's intricate and interconnected ecosystems is challenging. Alterations in one region will provoke alterations in others, significantly affecting wildlife.

Impact of Rising Temperatures

Globally rising temperatures are increasingly disrupting ecosystems, stressing wildlife, and intensifying weather patterns, with significant implications for biodiversity and human societies.

Habitat Loss

Increasing temperatures impact plant life, food availability, water accessibility, and other factors. These changes can make habitats unsuitable for some species, prompting them to seek sustenance and better living conditions elsewhere, disrupting normal migratory behaviors, or leading to their decline.

For instance, if the current pace of habitat destruction and division persists, exacerbated by human expansion and climate change, and if elephant poaching remains unchecked, Africa's elephant populations may vanish within four decades.

Natural Disasters

Today, the frequency of natural disasters related to climate and weather events, including droughts, wildfires, and hurricanes, has increased five times compared to half a century ago. Such calamities result in devastating losses for wildlife, human populations, and household animals.

Take the Black Summer bushfires in Australia (2019–2020) as an example: they scorched an area of 186,000 square kilometers (72,000 square miles), leading to the death or displacement of an estimated three billion animals, including koalas and kangaroos (*The Impact of Climate Change on Our Planet's Animals*, 2022).

Human-Wildlife Conflict

Climate change exacerbates the clash between humans and wildlife by shrinking habitats and magnifying the severity of climate phenomena, pushing both species into ever-tighter quarters. As habitats evolve, humans and animals must venture farther afield to secure food, water, and necessities. These confrontations typically have dire consequences for the wildlife involved.

For instance, when jaguars hunt livestock, they interfere with human economic activities, often prompting retaliatory killings. Such actions contribute to the accelerating reduction of the already endangered jaguar populations.

Extinction

The convergence of various threats may drive numerous species to extinction, with the animals most at risk, especially those nearing the end, likely to face the most significant dangers.

Take the North Atlantic right whale as a case in point: it is perilously close to extinction, with an estimated population of only 336, marking a twenty-year low. Rising ocean temperatures, alongside continued human conflicts like collisions with ships and entanglement in fishing equipment, could lead to the species' demise (*The Impact of Climate Change on Our Planet's Animals*, 2022).

While the plight of species like the North Atlantic right whale underscores the stark dangers of climate change, it's essential to recognize the positive flip side: animals are also part of the solution. Their roles in ecosystems offer a natural means to mitigate climate impacts, an aspect we will explore.

HOW ANIMALS CAN HELP CLIMATE CHANGE

We possess a formidable defense against climate change: animals and their ecosystems. The United Nations has calculated that intact ecosystems might contribute 37 percent of the carbon reduction required to curb global warming (*The Impact of Climate Change on Our Planet's Animals*, 2022).

Healthy Ecosystems Absorb and Store Carbon

Ecosystems teeming with flora capture and sequester carbon dioxide from the air. Hence, the conservation and restoration of natural habitats stand as a potent strategy in the urgent quest to halt climate change. Beyond carbon storage, these ecosystems also purify water, shield against floods, lessen disaster impacts, enhance soil quality, and nurture biodiversity. Keystone species, along with a myriad of other animals, hold crucial and sometimes unseen roles in maintaining biodiversity and habitat integrity.

Whales Play a Powerful Function in Sustaining Healthy Marine Ecosystems

For instance, whales bolster the health of marine ecosystems through their feces, which fertilize phytoplankton. These microscopic plants absorb CO_2 on a grand scale and transform it into energy, thereby extracting carbon from the atmosphere. This carbon is then cycled through the marine food chain, for example, when whales consume organisms that have fed on phytoplankton, ensuring that it remains sequestered.

Elephants Clear Ground Space to Encourage New Plant Growth

Elephants are ecosystem engineers; they scatter seeds, enrich the soil, create water sources, forge paths other creatures use, and clear vegetation to spur new growth, all contributing to ecosystems capable of locking away CO_2.

Pangolins Regulate Ants and Termites

Pangolins consume ants and termites to help regulate these insects' populations and dig out dens that become habitats for other species, playing a critical part in their ecological communities. Countless other animals fulfill equally vital functions within their respective ecosystems.

While animals and ecosystems are pivotal in mitigating climate change, pinpointing accountability for the accelerating crisis reveals a complex web of historical emissions, corporate influence, and policy decisions. Now, let's examine the entities and actions at the heart of the climate dilemma.

WHO IS TO BLAME?

Climate change manifests in everyday occurrences, with California's heat waves and Pakistan's floods displacing individuals and exacerbating global hunger and scarcity of food.

However, the climate crisis is uneven in its impact and accountability. Recent research by Oxfam shows that the carbon footprint of each of the 125 billionaires is a million times larger than that of an average person (*Who Is Responsible for Climate Change*, 2022).

Companies That Significantly and Negatively Contribute to Climate Change

Fossil fuel corporations have drastically driven climate change by persistently extracting fuels, a continuation of the Global North's history of pollution. Exposed by FRONTLINE, Exxon-Mobil disregarded its own 1980s research showing fossil fuels' role in global warming (Edge, 2022).

These companies, with government backing, have significantly released carbon dioxide and methane, contributing to 71 percent of emissions since 1988 (*New Report Shows Just 100 Companies Are Source of Over 70% of Emissions*, 2017). Despite a 1990s consensus on humans influencing climate change, oil lobbyists like the American Petroleum Institute strategically spread doubt, hindering progress on climate policies globally.

Rich Industrialized Countries Have Been the Primary Contributors to Emissions Causing Climate Change

The global divide in living standards, once relatively narrow, ballooned with the Industrial Revolution led by the Global North until the mid-twentieth century, which has had lasting climate impacts. The New York Times analysis reveals that twenty-three wealthy nations are responsible for 50 percent of historical carbon emissions, with the rest spread across over 150 countries (Plumer & Popovich, 2021).

James Hansen, a former NASA scientist, notes that between 1751 and 2006, the bulk of emissions originated from Europe, North America, Australia, and Japan, accounting for 77 percent of global emissions. Despite China's current position as the top emitter, the collective emissions of these wealthy nations still surpass a third of the worldwide total, whereas Africa's share is under 4 percent (Adow, 2020).

These developed countries are overwhelmingly accountable for the climate crisis. They must take decisive action by cutting their emissions and supporting developing countries in their transition to clean energy and climate resilience.

How the Richest People Contribute to Climate Change

Wealthy individuals also carry a notable share of the burden of climate change. Their affluent lifestyles aside, these "carbon billionaires" significantly fund large-scale polluters, Oxfam's research indicates.

The research identifies 125 billionaires channeling more than $2.4 trillion into 183 companies known for high carbon emissions, with the resultant pollution equating to the annual emissions of France (Maitland et al., 2022).

From 1990 to 2015, a period of sharp increase in the severity of the climate crisis, the carbon output from the top one percent of the wealthiest was over twice that of the bottom 50 percent of the global population. During the same quarter-century, this poorer half of humanity—approximately 3.1 billion people—contributed a mere 7 percent to total emissions (Maitland et al., 2022).

Countries That Have Benefited from the Use of Fossil Fuels and
Have Made the Most Significant Contributions to Climate Change

In 2021, greenhouse gas emissions soared to unprecedented levels, with fossil fuel carbon dioxide emissions hitting 36 billion metric tons (Crownhart, 2022). China is the top emitter, with the U.S. and the European Union following closely, and India and Russia contributing significantly.

However, current emissions don't fully capture a nation's climate impact. Due to carbon dioxide's long lifespan in the atmosphere, historical emissions are crucial to consider. By this measure, the U.S. emerges as the dominant historical emitter, accountable for more than 20 percent of total emissions, with the E.U. not far behind (Crownhart, 2022). When evaluating cumulative emissions, China's contribution is around half that of the U.S.

The substantial early emissions from the U.S. and E.U., linked to their longstanding reliance on fossil fuels, have been integral to their economic growth. This historical context places these regions at the forefront of debates over climate-related loss and damage. The world's wealthiest nations have had, and still maintain, a disproportionately significant influence on the climate.

Consumers versus Corporations

Climate change is a formidable global challenge, with fervent activists calling for urgent action. While people often promote sustainable practices and eco-friendly consumer habits, they overlook that corporations are the primary drivers of carbon emissions.

The Disproportionate Impact of Corporate Emissions

Research has revealed that since 1988, a mere 100 companies have produced 71 percent of the world's greenhouse gas emissions. Furthermore, a concentrated group of 25 companies and state enterprises are responsible for more than half of global industrial emissions (Waugh, 2022). These figures suggest that corporations should bear significant responsibility for climate action.

The Consumer versus Corporation Responsibility Debate

While much climate action focuses on individual lifestyle choices, such as purchasing sustainable products, using public transportation, and adopting plant-based diets, these solutions can overlook those who cannot afford or access these alternatives. With eco-friendly products often costing considerably more and some regions needing more public transportation infrastructure, only some have the liberty to make these green choices.

The Feasibility of Corporate Change

Corporations can make substantial changes toward sustainability by altering their operations. However, the predominant corporate focus on profit over the planet raises concerns. Companies like Exxon have known about climate change for years but have chosen to obstruct emission-reduction efforts.

Corporate Greenwashing and Political Hypocrisy

Some companies promote clean energy, but their investments suggest otherwise. For example, BP's extensive advertising of cleaner energy initiatives contrasts with their continued heavy investment in oil and gas. Politicians, too, can exhibit hypocrisy, advocating for climate solutions while engaging in environmentally harmful practices, undermining the message of responsibility and change.

The Fashion Industry's Climate Burden

The fashion sector, as the second-largest industrial polluter, contributes to 10 percent of global emissions (Waugh, 2022). Sustainable fashion remains financially out of reach for many, pushing them toward more affordable fast fashion options. The environmental effect of fast fashion is substantial, yet it's not typically the working class who contributes to overconsumption, a critical factor in the industry's carbon footprint.

Accountability for Climate Action

Corporations must acknowledge and act upon their substantial role in the climate crisis. With corporate accountability and transformative action, efforts to combat climate change may stay strong despite the burdens placed on consumers to drive change.

As corporations grapple with their responsibility, the effectiveness of global climate agreements comes under scrutiny. We will now evaluate the success and challenges of international pacts in uniting the world toward a sustainable and carbon-neutral future.

GLOBAL CLIMATE AGREEMENTS: HOW SUCCESSFUL ARE THEY?

For decades, world governments have vowed to decelerate the pace of global warming, but despite these diplomatic efforts, the impacts of climate change are unfolding and projected to intensify.

The world, through initiatives like the Kyoto Protocol and the Paris Agreement, has seen nations commit to curbing greenhouse gas emissions. Nevertheless, atmospheric carbon dioxide levels continue to climb, fueling a concerning rate of global heating. Experts caution that, without a course change, the planet may face dire consequences, such as drastic sea-level rises, extreme weather events, and extensive biodiversity loss.

After establishing the Paris Agreement in 2015, the countries involved have revisited and often increased their climate pledges at the yearly U.N. climate summits, known as COP. Still, in the lead-up to COP28 in Dubai, the U.N. has issued a stark reminder that the collective actions taken so far fall short of the necessary targets, calling for more rigorous efforts toward decarbonization.

The Most Influential Global Accords on Climate Change

International climate agreements are pivotal milestones in our collective effort to address global warming. Here are some of the critical accords that lay the foundation for coordinated action:

The 1987 Montreal Protocol

The Montreal Protocol of 1987, though not initially aimed at climate change, became a hallmark of environmental diplomacy as every nation in the world agreed to phase out substances depleting the ozone layer, such as chlorofluorocarbons (CFCs).

- **Effectiveness of the 1987 Montreal Protocol**

This treaty has successfully phased out almost 99 percent of these harmful compounds (Maizland, 2023). In 2016, the signatories committed to reducing hydrofluorocarbon (HFCs), potent contributors to global warming, through the Kigali Amendment.

The 1992 United Nations Framework Convention on Climate Change (UNFCCC)

In 1992, the UNFCCC emerged as the first global treaty to focus on climate change, ratified by 197 nations, including the United States. It set up a yearly conference, the Conference of Parties (COP), to foster international dialogue on maintaining greenhouse gas levels in the atmosphere. This forum led to the creation of the Kyoto Protocol and the Paris Agreement.

- **Effectiveness of the 1992 UNFCCC**

The effectiveness of the UNFCCC lies in its role as a platform for dialogue, commitment, and establishing regulatory frameworks to combat climate change. However, translating commitments into action remains a persistent challenge, as nations need help to meet agreed-upon targets, and the pace of global emissions reductions still needs to catch up to what is required to limit catastrophic warming.

The 1997 Kyoto Protocol

The Kyoto Protocol, adopted in 1997 but effective in 2005, marked the first binding climate agreement, demanding that developed nations cut emissions by 5 percent from 1990 levels and install a system for tracking their progress (Maizland, 2023). However, it didn't mandate emission cuts from expanding countries like India and China. The U.S. signed but never ratified the treaty and ultimately withdrew its signature.

- **Effectiveness of the 1997 Kyoto Protocol**

The Kyoto Protocol represented a pivotal step in international climate policy, obligating industrialized nations to reduce emissions, thereby setting a precedent for future agreements. Its effectiveness, however, was limited by the absence of binding commitments by emerging economies such as China and India and the United States' decision to neither ratify nor adhere to the treaty, significantly undermining its global impact.

The 2015 Paris Agreement

The Paris Agreement in 2015 stands as the most comprehensive global climate pact, necessitating that all participating countries outline emissions reduction plans to cap global temperature rises to 2 °C past pre-industrial levels and ideally below 1.5 °C, aiming for a net-zero emission balance by the latter half of the twenty-first century (Maizland, 2023).

Countries must reassess their progress every five years in a "global stocktake." The first evaluation, in September 2023, indicated that global efforts are falling short of the Paris Agreement's long-term objectives.

The U.S., the second-highest emitter, briefly exited the agreement under President Donald Trump in November 2020, but President Joe Biden reinstated the nation soon after taking office. As of now, Iran, Libya, and Yemen have yet to join the agreement formally.

- **Effectiveness of the 2015 Paris Agreement**

With major emitters like Iran outside the accord, the agreement's global efficacy is tempered, signaling a need for all-inclusive participation and intensified ambitions to bridge the gap between current trajectories and the pact's aspirations.

As nations confront the shortfall in meeting Paris Agreement targets, the critical threshold of a 1.5 °C temperature cap emerges as a global focal point, underpinning strategies to avert the most severe impacts of climate change. We explore the rationale behind this specific temperature goal.

Why Countries Are Aiming to Keep the Global Temperature Rise Below 1.5 Degrees

For years, scientists have sounded alarms about the dire environmental fallout if global temperatures persist on their upward trajectory. The Earth has heated by approximately 1.1 °C beyond pre-industrial times, per a 2021 Intergovernmental Panel on Climate Change (IPCC) assessment authored by over 200 scientists from more than 60 nations.

This report forecasts that the planet will probably hit or surpass 1.5 °C of warming in the next twenty years, despite immediate drastic emission reductions by countries (*Global Warming of 1.5 °C*, n.d.).

The IPCC has also detailed the devastating consequences of a 1.5 °C increase in global temperatures:

- Frequent heat waves will afflict various regions, subjecting approximately 14 percent of the global population to extreme heat every five years.
- Increased risk of droughts and floods will challenge agriculture, diminishing crop production and leading to food scarcity.
- Rising sea levels will endanger tens of millions living in coastal areas, with small island nations facing acute risks.
- Ocean ecosystems will see up to 90 percent of coral reefs destroyed and increased acidity, impacting fish stocks.

- The Arctic is poised to lose its summer sea ice occasionally, a phenomenon not seen in over 2,000 years, and will see significant permafrost melt.
- An upsurge in the extinction risk for various insects, plants, and vertebrate species (*Global Warming of 1.5 ᵒC*, n.d.).

Scientists warn that these impacts will intensify if temperatures climb to 2 °C (*Global Warming of 1.5 ᵒC*, n.d.).

KEY TAKEAWAYS

- The Earth's temperature has increased by 1.1 °C since the nineteenth century, and scientists project it will increase by 2.7 °C by the end of the century, causing impacts on ecosystems and wildlife.
- Rising temperatures lead to habitat loss, disrupt migratory patterns, and threaten species like elephants and jaguars.
- Natural catastrophes related to climate change, such as wildfires and cyclones, are becoming more frequent and devastating for humans and wildlife.
- Climate change exacerbates human-wildlife conflicts, as shrinking habitats force both species to compete for resources, leading to negative consequences for wildlife.
- Animals and ecosystems can help mitigate climate change by sequestering carbon and supporting healthy ecosystems.

- Complex factors contributing to climate change include historical emissions, corporate influence, and policy decisions.
- The wealthiest people have a considerably more extensive carbon footprint than the regular individual.
- Fossil fuel corporations and rich industrialized nations have been the primary historical contributors to climate change.
- Corporations need to take substantial steps toward sustainability and reducing emissions.
- Global climate accords like the Kyoto Protocol and the Paris Agreement have progressed, but global emissions continue to rise.
- The Montreal Protocol successfully phased out harmful compounds, while the Kyoto Protocol had limitations due to a lack of commitments from developing countries and the U.S. withdrawal.
- The Paris Agreement seeks to restrict global temperature rise to 1.5 °C, but many countries are falling short of their targets.
- Controlling the rise of global temperatures to below 1.5 °C is crucial to avoid severe impacts, including heat waves, food scarcity, rising sea levels, coral reef destruction, and extinction risks.

While the challenges of climate change and its impact on wildlife are significant, it's essential to remember that positive change is possible. Next, we explore these strategies and inspiring stories to empower ourselves for effective wildlife conservation.

8

CHANGING THE NEXT GENERATION

"It seems to me that the natural world is the greatest source of excitement; the greatest source of visual beauty; the greatest source of intellectual interest. It is the greatest source of so much in life that makes life worth living."

— DAVID ATTENBOROUGH

David Attenborough expresses that nature fuels our joy, inspires our aesthetics, and stimulates our minds. It enriches life, making it fulfilling. This highlights the critical need for ongoing wildlife conservation to secure the preservation of these natural wonders and knowledge for future generations.

THE FUTURE OF WILDLIFE CONSERVATION

Recognition is growing for the essential role of wildlife conservation in promoting sustainability, enhancing health, and fighting against poverty and hunger. The Convention on International Trade in Endangered Species of Wild Fauna and Flora (CITES) Convention and subsequent initiatives have succeeded in things such as recovering the vicuña population in the Andes, leading to sustainable trade practices.

Conservation efforts like those in Bolivia and Australia have proven economically beneficial while preserving species. Conservation practices ensure food security through forest protection and carbon sequestration and maintain agricultural diversity, which is vital in preventing zoonotic diseases by acting as a buffer between wildlife and humans.

Recognizing the pivotal role of wildlife conservation in global well-being, we turn to innovative methods like digital habitat simulations. These virtual ecosystems enable us to predict and strategize for biodiversity protection, intertwining technology with natural preservation efforts.

Creating Simulations with Digital Habitats

Pat Zollner, a scientific researcher, leads a team of graduate students delving into diverse ecological studies, from black vulture behavior to disease impacts on bats and deer, primate management in West Africa, and conservation of the least Bell's vireo in California. They use agent-based modeling to create and analyze digital ecosystems, simulating real-world animal behaviors in various environmental scenarios.

This innovative approach aids in forecasting how different forest management plans affect species like the American marten, which is essential for advising the National Forest Service on strategies for species sustainability. Rob Swihart, another critical researcher, underscores the necessity of rigorous data collection in wildlife management. His four-year analysis has been pivotal for the Indiana Department of Natural Resources in deer management.

Swihart and Zollner's collaboration extended to evaluating bobcat habitats, enhanced by computer scientist David Gleich's computational methods, leading to groundbreaking insights into habitat sustainability.

As Zollner and Swihart exemplify the integration of technology and ecology, we look ahead to cutting-edge technologies poised to revolutionize wildlife conservation, transforming how we protect and sustain the natural world through advanced computational methods and innovative data analysis.

Cutting-Edge Technologies That Can Revolutionize Wildlife Conservation

Earth is home to an estimated 8.7 million species, yet a staggering 86 percent of land species and 91 percent of ocean species remain undiscovered (Chu Minh, 2022). Studies warn that without intervention, biodiversity faces a severe threat, with the potential for up to half of all species to become extinct by this century's end.

Traditional methods for monitoring biodiversity, such as camera traps and aerial surveys, have proven resource-intensive and costly. However, the emergence of cutting-edge technologies promises to revolutionize wildlife conservation efforts.

Using Artificial Intelligence and Public Participation in Identifying Wildlife

Artificial Intelligence (AI) plays an increasingly crucial function in analyzing vast conservation datasets, including camera trap images, satellite and drone imagery, and audio and video recordings. The non-profit organization Wild Me has developed Wildbook, a cloud-based platform powered by computer vision and deep learning algorithms.

Wildbook scans millions of crowdsourced wildlife images, identifying species and individual animals based on distinctive physical characteristics, such as stripes, spots, or scars. Scientists, volunteers, and social media users contribute images, enriching the platform's species database. This aggregated data informs conservation efforts and engages the public in tracking their favorite animals.

Facial Recognition for Wildlife Conservation

The BearID Project is pioneering facial recognition software for wildlife conservation. This technology fills a critical gap left by camera traps, which struggle to consistently identify individual bears due to the absence of distinct natural markings for some species.

The project has developed an AI system using personal photographs of brown bears. This system achieved an impressive 84 percent accuracy rate in identifying 132 individual bears (Chu Minh, 2022). While still in development, the project aims to expand the software's applicability to other endangered species.

AI for Anti-Poaching Efforts

AI can significantly bolster anti-poaching initiatives. The Protection Assistant for Wildlife Security (PAWS) software uses past poaching records and geographic data to predict poachers' future behavior, generating poaching risk maps and optimal patrol routes for rangers.

In a field test at the Srepok Wildlife Sanctuary in Cambodia, PAWS helped rangers double the detection and removal of snares during patrols. Integration with the Spatial Monitoring and Reporting Tool (SMART) enhances data collection and produces poaching risk maps. Plans include connecting PAWS to remote sensing tools like satellites and drones, broadening its scope to predict other environmental crimes.

Environmental DNA (eDNA) for Biodiversity Monitoring

Environmental DNA (eDNA) provides a game-changing method for collecting biodiversity data. By extracting DNA from ecological samples like water, soil, snow, or air, eDNA captures traces left by all living organisms. A single model can offer a comprehensive snapshot of an entire ecosystem, providing insights that can surpass the capabilities of camera traps.

Recent studies have demonstrated that eDNA sampling detected 25 percent more terrestrial mammal species at half the cost (Chu Minh, 2022). This technology also enables the assessment of climate change impacts, the detection of invisible threats like viruses or bacteria, and the evaluation of overall ecosystem health.

Enhancing Connectivity for Improved Conservation Outcomes

Networked sensors offer a comprehensive view of animal behavior and immediate alerts about threats, enhancing monitoring and patrolling efforts. Initiatives like FieldKit and the Arribada Initiative focus on developing low-cost, open-source sensor systems, while Smart Parks and Sensing Clues optimize protected area monitoring through networked sensors.

Smart Parks' technology, operating autonomously on solar power, has been deployed in protected areas globally. These sensors track data from human intrusions to animal breaches, facilitating anti-poaching efforts and mitigating human-wildlife conflicts.

Leveraging Games for Wildlife Conservation

Beyond traditional tools, engaging the tech-savvy younger generation in conservation is crucial. The Internet of Elephants develops gaming and digital experiences based on scientific data to draw individuals into wildlife conservation. Products like Wildeverse and Unseen Empire use real-life camera trap imagery to educate players about the impact of deforestation, poaching, and other human activities on endangered wildlife.

Addressing Inequalities in Conservation Technology

While these technologies hold immense promise, they also reveal challenges within the conservation tech ecosystem. These include competition for limited funding, duplicated efforts, and insufficient capacity-building. The research highlights that these challenges disproportionately impact women and people in developing countries.

Programs that merge technology with conservation efforts are emerging, enabling local communities to develop and apply technological solutions for conservation. By fostering local capacity-building, these programs ensure the long-term effectiveness and sustainability of conservation solutions.

In an era where biodiversity is under dire threat, integrating innovative technologies offers a glimmer of hope for wildlife conservation. These transformative tools, powered by AI, citizen science, and eDNA, hold the potential to revolutionize how we monitor, protect, and understand the natural world.

Moreover, by addressing inequalities and fostering local capacity-building, these technologies can contribute to a more inclusive and sustainable approach to wildlife conservation.

Amidst these technological strides in global wildlife conservation, we also recognize the power of individual actions. Now, let's focus on the manageable steps each of us can take within our homes to contribute to more extensive environmental preservation efforts.

TAKING ACTION: MAKING SMALL DIFFERENCES AT HOME

Biodiversity encompasses not just the variety of life forms but also the ecological systems that support them. Although safeguarding vast areas like rainforests may seem overwhelming, here's a list of how you can contribute significantly to the enhancement and conservation of biodiversity right from your own home:

1. **Support Local Agriculture:** Invest in your community by purchasing from local farmers at markets or through Community Supported Agriculture subscriptions. This approach strengthens the local economy and maintains farming practices that safeguard biodiversity. Seek out products labeled "organic" or "Integrated Pest Management" for environmentally friendly options.
2. **Protect the Bees:** Aid bee populations by planting wildflowers that provide nectar and by constructing bee boxes. Be cautious of pesticides in home gardening projects, as they can harm these crucial pollinators.
3. **Grow Native Plants:** Contribute to local ecosystems by planting indigenous flowers, fruits, and vegetables. Consult and patronize local nurseries for advice and supply of native plant species, ensuring the support of regional wildlife and biodiversity.
4. **Conserve Water:** Save local water resources essential for biodiversity by reducing shower time and turning off taps when not in active use, like brushing teeth or dishwashing.

5. **Preserve Natural Areas:** Maintain the integrity of local habitats by staying on designated paths in parks and nature reserves, and encouraging children and pets to follow suit, safeguarding the native ecosystem.

6. **Make Conscious Purchases:** When purchasing products, seek out eco-friendly options with certifications like FSC or Rainforest Alliance. This helps to prevent habitat loss and supports the rights of Indigenous peoples in resource-harvesting areas.

7. **Distinguish At-Risk Species:** Teach students the critical differences between endangered, threatened, and rare species using PLT's free resources, helping them understand the severe impacts of biodiversity loss.

8. **Support Bird Populations:** Encourage ecosystem balance by setting up bird feeders, attracting various birds that pollinate plants, and controlling insect populations. Use resources like Cornell's Project FeederWatch to monitor and maintain bird feeder hygiene to prevent diseases.

9. **Construct Nesting Boxes:** Increase bird diversity by building nesting boxes, tapping into Cornell's NestWatch for guidance on creating and placing birdhouses effectively, and participating in citizen science by reporting sightings.

10. **Facilitate Bat Conservation:** Help bats, crucial for pollination and insect control, by installing bat houses. Learn from Bat Conservation International and celebrate bats with educational activities during Bat Week.

11. **Create Homes for Pollinators:** Boost bee and butterfly numbers by constructing pollinator houses tailored to local species, ensuring design research to provide safe and effective habitats.

12. **Plant Native Species:** Enhance local biodiversity by planting native flora. Involve children in gardening projects, emphasizing the ecological importance of native plants over non-native species.

13. **Avoid Pesticides:** Maintain a pesticide-free garden, opting for compost to nourish the soil and support a healthy ecosystem for plants, worms, and beneficial microorganisms.

As we recognize these individual contributions to biodiversity at home, let's shift our attention to the broader canvas. We'll explore the success stories of the century, highlighting triumphs in conservation and the restoration of ecosystems that continue to inspire global environmental stewardship.

SUCCESS STORIES OF THE CENTURY

The current century has brought significant obstacles and victories in the field of wildlife conservation globally. Destruction of habitats and unlawful hunting practices have endangered many species. Yet the relentless efforts of dedicated people, groups, and governments have been crucial in safeguarding and rejuvenating the world's most at-risk wildlife.

Through persistent and collaborative conservation methods, there is a potential to overturn the decline of these species and re-establish ecological equilibrium. Although the journey is intricate and gradual, it promises remarkable outcomes.

The Return of the Giant Panda

The giant panda's resurgence is a beacon of conservation success. In China, dedicated habitat protection and the creation of nature reserves have provided a refuge for these animals, facilitating a rise in their population. Vigilant conservation efforts ensure pandas have access to abundant bamboo, their essential diet, with initiatives to replant and diversify bamboo forests.

This strategy has rejuvenated both the pandas' diet and their habitat. International partnerships have amplified these endeavors, providing vital resources and fostering a global commitment to the panda's future, reinforcing its iconic status in wildlife conservation and garnering widespread support.

The Recovery of the Bald Eagle

During the mid-1900s, bald eagle numbers declined sharply due to dichlorodiphenyltrichloroethane (DDT) poisoning— which caused their eggs to be fragile—and habitat destruction from increasing urbanization. Recognizing the critical decline, the U.S. government announced the bald eagle as an endangered species in 1967, which was essential in halting its population decline (Heisman, 2018).

The subsequent ban on DDT was instrumental in their recovery, leading to population stabilization and habitat restoration.

In 2007, the culmination of practical conservation actions and legislation resulted in removing the bald eagle from the endangered species list (Heisman, 2018). Now, bald eagles are a frequent sight across various regions of the U.S., symbolizing a significant conservation triumph.

Stabilizing Black Rhino Populations

The black rhino, once nearing extinction due to illegal poaching and habitat destruction, has seen a reversal in fortunes, with populations now stabilizing and even increasing in some areas. A combination of concerted conservation efforts, vigorous anti-poaching campaigns, and community-driven conservation programs have been pivotal in this turnaround. The heightened demand for rhino horns, fueled by unfounded medicinal claims and their value as ornaments, had led to critical population declines.

Recent collaborative efforts among conservation bodies, local and international governments, and communities have protected the species. These programs have not only curtailed poaching activities but also instilled a sense of ownership and pride regarding wildlife stewardship within local communities.

In Namibia, such community-engaged conservation has proven effective, contributing significantly to the survival of the black rhino and offering a model for sustainable wildlife conservation.

The Bornean Rainbow Toad Reemerges

Believed extinct for eighty-seven years, the Bornean Rainbow Toad, or Sambas stream toad, was remarkably rediscovered in 2011, symbolizing nature's enduring tenacity. Initially documented in the 1920s and last seen in the mid-twentieth century, this toad, noted for its distinctive colors, had eluded detection (Boyle, 2011).

Dr. Indraneil Das's team undertook an arduous expedition into Borneo's dense rainforests (Boyle, 2011). Overcoming environmental challenges, the researchers located the toad at night, its vivid hues aiding in its identification and marking a significant moment in conservation history.

Combating Disease to Protect Tasmanian Devils

Efforts to rescue the Tasmanian devil from the brink of extinction are ongoing in Australia's wilderness. The species, once endangered by the rampant Devil Facial Tumor Disease, is now witnessing a potential resurgence, thanks to concerted efforts in disease management and conservation. Intensive research and strategic interventions have effectively curbed the disease's spread.

Through captive breeding programs, conservationists are preserving the genetic diversity of these unique marsupials and providing them with a haven for recovery. These measures act as a safeguard, ensuring the Tasmanian devil's survival and reflecting the relentless dedication to saving this iconic species.

The Revival of the California Condor

The California condor, a symbol of wildlife conservation, has experienced a significant recovery. From just twenty-two birds, the species' numbers have climbed to over 500, thanks to rigorous captive breeding and constant monitoring. The California condor, known for its vast 9.5-foot wingspan and distinctive looks, was on the verge of disappearing due to lead poisoning, loss of habitat, and environmental changes (*California Condor Reintroduction & Recovery*, 2017).

The pivotal moment arrived with the implementation of a captive breeding program. A committed team took on the challenge of saving these birds, breeding them in captivity with great care. This challenging task has yielded impressive results: the condor population is not only restored but is also flourishing. Presently, these enduring birds serve as an inspiring example of the power of focused commitment and the success of conservation efforts.

Gray Wolves Wander the Wilds Once More

Gray wolves have rebounded from the brink of extinction thanks to restoration efforts across North America. Once prevalent, by the early twentieth century, overhunting and habitat loss had severely depleted their populations. Conservationists championed their cause, recognizing their critical role as apex predators in maintaining ecosystems.

Resulting reintroduction programs have successfully restored wolves to their historic territories, notably in Yellowstone and the Northern Rockies. Their increasing presence has revived natural balances and renewed appreciation for the continent's wilderness, underscoring a significant wildlife conservation achievement.

Blue Whale Revival

Blue whales, the colossal denizens of the deep, have staged a comeback from near extinction due to historical whaling. Global conservation efforts, including the International Whaling Commission's commercial whaling ban and the creation of sanctuaries, have been pivotal in their recovery.

The WWF's support of the Ross Sea marine protected area in 2018, the largest to date, has been instrumental in safeguarding Antarctic blue whales. Additionally, the WWF actively advocates for comprehensive management of the Southern Ocean to counter overfishing, further promoting the ecological health of blue whale habitats.

The Humpback Whale's Resurgence

Humpback whales have remarkably recovered from the threat of extinction, overcoming historical overhunting that slashed their numbers by 90 percent. The International Whaling Commission's 1986 ban on humpback whaling and the establishment of Marine Protected Areas have been central to their resurgence (Mapes, 2023).

In the North Atlantic, their population grows 5 to 7 percent yearly (Mapes, 2023). Despite this success, ongoing threats like entanglement, ship strikes, and climate change persist. Continuous research, conservation efforts, and heightened public awareness are essential to sustain the humpback whale's revival.

The Arabian Oryx's Renewed Presence

Effective conservation strategies have enabled the once-extinct Arabian oryx to flourish once more in the deserts of the Middle East. Overhunting and environmental changes had nearly erased them by the 1970s. Captive breeding, supported by conservationists and governments, revived the species with the first reintroduction in Oman in 1982 (*Captive Breeding Success Stories*, 2009).

Ongoing efforts have established numerous protected areas across the Arabian Peninsula. As a result, the wild population of the Arabian oryx now surpasses 1,000, marking a significant victory for the species' preservation in its native habitat (*Captive Breeding Success Stories*, 2009).

Amidst these inspiring tales of wildlife resurgence, the call for passionate conservationists grows ever louder. Pursuing a career in wildlife conservation offers the chance to join this vital fight, safeguarding our planet's irreplaceable biodiversity for future generations and contributing to stories of ecological redemption.

PURSUING A CAREER IN WILDLIFE CONSERVATION

Pursuing a career in wildlife conservation is a noble and fulfilling path, combining a passion for the natural world with the imperative to protect it. This field offers diverse roles, from research to advocacy, each playing a part in safeguarding our planet's precious wildlife.

The Pros and Cons of a Career in Wildlife Conservation

Here are the benefits and drawbacks of pursuing a career in wildlife conservation:

Pros

1. **Meaningful Impact:** Engaging in conservation work allows you to contribute to protecting endangered species and ecosystems, making a tangible difference.
2. **Rewarding Experience:** There's a deep sense of fulfillment and achievement in knowing your efforts aid wildlife conservation on a national and global level.
3. **Diverse Opportunities:** Work in conservation varies widely, from preserving local species to participating in high-profile international projects, ensuring a dynamic and exciting job environment.
4. **Respect and Recognition:** A career in wildlife conservation is esteemed globally, honoring the dedication to preserving animals and their habitats.

Cons

1. **Not Always Glamorous:** The job includes routine tasks that are not exciting, such as fence checking and vegetation management, which are crucial but less appealing aspects of the role.
2. **Financial Limitations:** Most conservation jobs are not highly paid, with funding often coming from government or charitable sources, making financial gain less likely.
3. **Challenging Work Conditions:** The work can sometimes be physically demanding and may require being in remote or difficult environments.

A career in wildlife conservation offers immense personal satisfaction and the opportunity for a significant impact, despite financial limitations and the presence of routine or physically demanding tasks.

How to Begin a Profession in Wildlife Conservation

1. **Dive into Volunteer Work:** Acquire hands-on experience and build professional connections through volunteer work. Activities could range from habitat restoration to species tracking and public education, often leading to professional roles.
2. **Engage in Research and Field Work:** Participate in data collection and analysis by joining research projects or fieldwork. Paid roles and internships are offered by institutions such as the Rainforest Alliance and the Jane

Goodall Institute, though they may require specific qualifications.

3. **Advance Your Education:** Pursue higher education and obtain the necessary credentials. Degrees in biology, environmental science, or wildlife management from institutions like the University of Minnesota or the University of Oxford can be crucial for a career in this field.

4. **Explore Internships:** For a hands-on conservation experience, consider GVI's internships. They provide training in diverse environments, from marine ecosystems to significant mammal habitats, and teach valuable research and community engagement skills.

Whether you volunteer, engage in fieldwork, further your education, or undertake an internship, each path offers a unique entry into the fulfilling world of wildlife conservation.

Occupations in Wildlife Preservation

Exploring jobs in wildlife conservation offers a gateway to careers dedicated to safeguarding our planet's diverse species. Consider exploring these job opportunities:

Entry-Level Positions

- **Outdoor Education Instructor:** Educates the public about the natural world and conservation efforts, often through guided tours and interactive programs.

- **Park Ranger:** Serves as a custodian of parks, ensuring the protection of wildlife and natural resources while facilitating visitor access and education.
- **Field Technician:** Conducts practical fieldwork, collecting data and samples that support wildlife research and management.
- **Wildlife Advocate:** Works to raise public awareness and influence policy to protect wildlife and its habitat.
- **Research Assistant:** Aids in scientific studies, helping to gather and analyze data on wildlife and ecological systems.
- **Wildlife Photographer:** Captures wildlife images in natural habitats to support conservation messages and education.
- **Habitat Restoration and Ecological Monitoring:** Involves repairing damaged ecosystems and tracking the health of wildlife populations and their habitats.
- **Conservation Journalist:** Reports on wildlife conservation issues, informing and engaging the public on the importance of biodiversity.

Mid- to Senior-Level Positions

- **Wildlife Biologist:** Studies animals and their interactions with ecosystems, often pivotal in developing conservation plans and policies.
- **Marine Biologist:** Specializes in ocean ecosystems, studying marine wildlife and contributing to maritime conservation strategies.

- **Entomologist:** Concentrates on entomological research to enhance knowledge of insect biodiversity and ecosystem vitality.
- **Wildlife Veterinarian:** Provides medical care to wildlife, often working within conservation programs to ensure the health of animal populations.
- **Herpetologist:** Studies reptiles and amphibians, providing insights crucial for conserving these often-sensitive species.
- **Wildlife Law Enforcement Officer:** Enforces laws and regulations that protect wildlife, combating poaching and illegal trade.
- **Environmental Scientist:** Investigates ecological issues, including wildlife impacts, to inform and develop conservation and restoration efforts.
- **Wildlife Researcher:** Conducts in-depth studies of wildlife, generating knowledge that underpins conservation initiatives.
- **Wildlife Filmmaker:** Creates visual narratives on wildlife and conservation, raising awareness and educating through documentaries and the media.

With a clear understanding of the roles available in wildlife conservation, let's now navigate the steps to secure a position in this vital field. We'll explore practical strategies to launch a successful career dedicated to preserving our natural world.

Ways to Secure a Career in Wildlife Conservation

1. **Volunteer Work Is Key:** Starting as a volunteer is crucial. It demonstrates commitment, provides essential hands-on experience, opens doors to job opportunities, and helps clarify career interests. However, these positions are competitive, so prepare for a rigorous selection process.
2. **Acquire Relevant Qualifications:** Those in top conservation roles are usually highly educated. Degrees in relevant fields are prevalent, but expertise in law, finance, or communication is also valuable. Tailored university courses and practical training programs can enhance prospects. Continuous learning and skill development are vital.
3. **Build a Professional Network:** Networking, rather than traditional advertising, often leads to job opportunities. Joining societies and attending conferences, especially in specialized subjects, can lead to job opportunities through networking.
4. **Professional Presentation Matters:** When applying for jobs, ensure applications are error-free and professional. A sloppy application can undermine your credibility.
5. **Persistence Pays Off, but Don't Overdo It:** Following up on job applications is good, but excessive contact can be counterproductive—respect potential employers' time and resources, including sending a self-addressed envelope when seeking responses.

KEY TAKEAWAYS

- Wildlife conservation is critical to sustainability and global health, with successful initiatives like CITES leading to sustainable trade and species recovery.
- Conservation efforts provide economic benefits and ensure food security by maintaining biodiversity and preventing zoonotic diseases.
- Wildlife conservationists use digital habitat simulations to forecast and strategize biodiversity protection, integrating technology with conservation efforts.
- Cutting-edge technologies like AI, facial recognition, and eDNA are revolutionizing wildlife conservation, improving species monitoring and anti-poaching efforts.
- Challenges in conservation tech, such as funding and capacity building, are being addressed to ensure inclusive and sustainable solutions.
- Taking personal steps, such as buying from local farmers and reducing pesticide use, boosts home biodiversity.
- The revival of diverse species through successful global conservation shows that restoration of ecological balance is achievable.
- Pursuing a career in wildlife conservation involves diverse roles and requires dedication, with entry-level positions like Outdoor Education Instructor and mid-level roles like Wildlife Biologist.

- To secure a career in conservation, volunteering, gaining relevant qualifications, networking, and professional presentation are crucial steps.
- Persistence is vital in job searches, but it's essential to balance follow-ups with respect for potential employers' resources.

MAKE A DIFFERENCE WITH YOUR REVIEW

Keeping the Conservation Legacy Alive

As you turn the final pages of "Wildlife Conservation Decoded," you're now armed with knowledge and insights that can make a real difference in our world. But remember, the journey doesn't end here.

Your thoughts and opinions about this book can help guide others who are just beginning their journey in wildlife conservation. By leaving your honest review on Amazon, you're not just critiquing a book; you're passing the torch of knowledge and passion for the environment.

Your review helps other enthusiasts find the guidance and inspiration they need to make their mark in conservation. It's a simple gesture, but it has the power to create a ripple effect, inspiring and educating others about the importance of preserving our natural world.

To leave your review, visit the following link or scan the QR code:

[https://www.amazon.com/review/review-your-purchases/?asin=B0CWYHG4R3]

Every review counts, and every opinion matters. Your contribution helps keep the conversation about wildlife conservation alive and thriving. You are now part of a community dedicated to safeguarding our planet for future generations.

Thank you for being a crucial part of this mission. Together, we are making a difference, one review, one reader, one conservationist at a time.

With heartfelt appreciation,

GoldenPedal Publishing

CONCLUSION

Conserving wildlife is essential to maintaining Earth's extensive array of life forms and the ecosystems that support them. Conservation aims to protect species and their habitats, which has become more urgent due to human activities that lead to habitat loss and endanger species. Conservation now focuses on entire ecosystems, building on the interconnectedness of species.

Conservation is pivotal in sustaining nature's delicate network, preserving the balance of life's complex interactions. The extinction of species, now occurring much faster than the natural background rate, highlights the delicacy of our natural world. However, initiatives like habitat restoration, sustainable practices, and genetic research offer hope for reversing the damage done to biodiversity.

Two primary fields underpin conservation efforts: conservation science, which adopts an expansive perspective that includes the social sciences and economics, and conservation biology, which centers on taking swift action to prevent the decline in biodiversity. Both fields employ strategies grounded in research and pragmatism, emphasizing the need for interdisciplinary collaboration.

One concern in conservation is the influence of large donors and corporations, which can sometimes lead to imbalances in funding and attention, often at the expense of less well-known species. Ensuring conservation efforts are balanced and holistic is essential for practical biodiversity preservation.

The vast array of life forms, spanning millions of known species with countless others awaiting discovery, is vital for the well-being of our planet and human life. Notably, biodiversity hotspots like Mexico, South Africa, and Madagascar play an essential role, with each species contributing valuable resources.

In the United States, recent studies have highlighted the risk of extinction for many species, with ecosystems under threat due to habitat loss, climate change, and insufficient conservation measures. Meeting the 2030 target to reverse biodiversity loss is a significant challenge, with strategies like sustainable agriculture and expanding protected areas offering a glimmer of hope.

Agricultural practices significantly impact biodiversity, affecting soil quality, climate, and food security. Sustainable practices such as agroecology and dietary changes can help preserve biodiversity. Additionally, wildlife management is necessary to balance animal populations and their habitats, with techniques ranging from habitat manipulation to population control. However, ethical considerations must be taken into account, particularly in urban areas.

Reintroducing species to their native habitats and rewilding with large predators are essential strategies for restoring ecological balance. These efforts have shown success, but they require careful management of stakeholder conflicts.

Disease management in wildlife is vital to protect species from decline and humans from zoonotic diseases, with strategies that include prevention, vaccination, and eradication.

Climate change poses a substantial danger to wildlife, causing habitat loss and increasing conflicts. The main contributors to climate change are fossil fuel companies and the consumption patterns of wealthy nations and individuals.

Technology plays a pivotal role in wildlife conservation, with advancements like digital simulations, AI, facial recognition, and environmental DNA transforming how we monitor and protect species. It's crucial to captivate young minds with educational games that teach conservation, though we must also confront obstacles such as financial constraints and social disparities.

Taking individual steps toward conservation, like bolstering local ecosystems, safeguarding pollinators, and cultivating native flora, can have a substantial impact. The resurgence of numerous wildlife populations is a testament to the effectiveness of sustained conservation endeavors.

Embarking on a career in wildlife conservation offers an enriching experience, demanding not just dedication and specialized knowledge but also a collaborative spirit to join forces with like-minded professionals.

Start making a difference in wildlife conservation by educating others—this is where you can ignite a transformative change for the next generation. Share the reality of our planet's rich biodiversity and its precarious state. Highlight how every species and habitat is a crucial thread in the tapestry of life, which we are responsible for safeguarding. Emphasize the urgency of combating habitat destruction and species endangerment caused by our actions.

Lead by example: champion sustainable practices and support local ecosystems. Teach the importance of pollinators by creating habitats for them in your community. Advocate for adopting agroecological methods and dietary shifts to reduce the strain on our environment. Underline the critical role that conscientious management of wildlife plays in sustaining the balance within ecosystems.

Encourage participation in species reintroduction programs and support rewilding efforts that restore the natural order. Highlight the imperative of managing diseases in wildlife populations to safeguard the health of animals and humans alike. Make it clear that combating climate change is non-negotiable for the survival of countless species, including our own.

Use technological advances to enhance public consciousness about important issues. Use digital platforms, AI, and innovative tools to track and share the progress of conservation efforts. Inspire youth by integrating educational games that teach the principles of ecology and conservation.

You have the power to contribute to the recovery of wildlife populations. Take action, inspire others to follow suit, and pursue a path in wildlife conservation if your passion lies there. Collectively, we can protect our planet's biodiversity for the wonder and enjoyment of future generations. Act now, educate continuously, and collaborate widely—our wildlife depends on it.

REFERENCES

Adow, M. (2020, April 13). *The Climate Debt the West Owes the Rest*. Foreign Affairs. https://www.foreignaffairs.com/articles/world/2020-04-13/climate-debt

Alagona, P. (2015, July 1). *How City Dwellers Can Live in Harmony With Urban Wildlife*. The New Republic. https://newrepublic.com/article/122219/how-city-dwellers-can-live-harmony-urban-wildlife

Alexander, N. (n.d.). *The Wonder and Future of Wildlife Conservation – Envision – College of Agriculture Magazine at Purdue University*. Purdue Agriculture. https://ag.purdue.edu/envision/the-wonder-and-future-of-wildlife-conservation/

Aninta, G. (2020, November 10). *A Beginner's Guide to Endangered Species Reintroduction*. Ecology for the Masses. https://ecologyforthemasses.com/2020/11/10/a-beginners-guide-to-endangered-species-reintroduction/

Attenborough, D. (n.d.). *David Attenborough - The question is, are we happy to...* Brainy Quote. https://www.brainyquote.com/quotes/david_attenborough_214799

Bar-on, Y. M., Phillips, R., & Milo, R. (2018, May 21). The biomass distribution on Earth. *The Proceedings of the National Academy of Sciences, 115*(25), 6506-6511. https://doi.org/10.1073/pnas.1711842115

Bennett, E. (2020, October 1). *9 animals facing extinction due to the loss of their habitats*. Trafalgar Tours. https://www.trafalgar.com/real-word/9-animals-facing-extinction-habitat-loss/

Biodiversity. (2023, October 19). National Geographic Society. https://education.nationalgeographic.org/resource/biodiversity/

Biodiversity and Agriculture. (2021, February 17). FoodPrint. https://foodprint.org/issues/biodiversity-and-agriculture/

Biodiversity in Focus: United States Edition. (2023, February 6). NatureServe. https://www.natureserve.org/bif

Boyce, M. S., & Byrne, R. L. (n.d.). *Managing Predator-Prey Systems: Summary Discussion*. Wildlife Management Institute. https://wildlifemanagement.institute/sites/default/files/2016-09/19-Summary_Discussion.pdf

Boyle, A. (2011, July 13). *'Lost' rainbow toad rediscovered*. NBC News. https://

www.nbcnews.com/science/cosmic-log/lost-rainbow-toad-rediscovered-flna6c10402999

California Condor Reintroduction & Recovery. (2017, January 25). National Park Service. https://www.nps.gov/articles/california-condor-recovery.htm

Campbell, R., Dutton, A., & Hughes, J. (2007, November). *Economic Impacts of the Beaver.* ResearchGate. https://www.researchgate.net/publication/261727410_Economic_Impacts_of_the_Beaver

Captive Breeding Success Stories. (2009, April 1). PBS. https://www.pbs.org/wnet/nature/the-loneliest-animals-captive-breeding-success-stories/4920/

Chu Minh, T. (2022, February 4). *These new technologies could transform wildlife conservation.* The Hill. https://thehill.com/changing-america/sustainability/environment/592820-these-new-technologies-could-transform-wildlife/

Crownhart, C. (2022, November 18). *Who's responsible for climate change? Three charts explain.* MIT Technology Review. https://www.technologyreview.com/2022/11/18/1063443/responsible-climate-change-charts/

D., L. (2023, October 7). *Top 10 Wildlife Conservation Success Stories of the Century.* Listverse. https://listverse.com/2023/10/07/top-10-wildlife-conservation-success-stories-of-the-century/

Danby, I. (n.d.). *Reintroductions: good or bad?* BASC. https://basc.org.uk/reintroductions-good-or-bad/

David Attenborough - It seems to me that the natural world... (n.d.). Brainy Quote. https://www.brainyquote.com/quotes/david_attenborough_214808

Drivers of Biodiversity Loss: Overexploitation. (2022, December 8). Defenders of Wildlife. https://defenders.org/blog/2022/12/drivers-of-biodiversity-loss-overexploitation

Edge, D. (2022, April 19). *The Power of Big Oil.* PBS. https://www.pbs.org/wgbh/frontline/documentary/the-power-of-big-oil/

Examining the Impacts of Disease on Wildlife Conservation and Management. (2019, October 16). U.S. Fish and Wildlife Service. https://www.fws.gov/testimony/examining-impacts-disease-wildlife-conservation-and-management

Explainer: Can the world 'halt and reverse' biodiversity loss by 2030? (2023, January 16). Carbon Brief. https://www.carbonbrief.org/explainer-can-the-world-halt-and-reverse-biodiversity-loss-by-2030/

Extinction Over Time | Smithsonian National Museum of Natural History. (n.d.). Smithsonian National Museum of Natural History. https://naturalhistory.si.edu/education/teaching-resources/paleontology/extinction-over-time

5 Threats To Biodiversity and How We Can Counter Them. (2023, July 24).

Defenders of Wildlife. https://defenders.org/blog/2023/07/5-threats-biodi
versity-and-how-we-can-counter-them

Four ways to reverse nature loss by 2030 for people and planet. (2022, April 1). WWF
Updates. https://updates.panda.org/four-ways-to-reverse-nature-loss-by-
2030

Genetic research boosts conservation efforts for critically endangered antelope | RZSS.
(2023, April 13). Royal Zoological Society of Scotland. https://www.rzss.
org.uk/news/article/21834/genetic-research-boosts-conservation-efforts-
for-critically-endangered-antelope/

Global Warming of 1.5 ºC. (n.d.). IPCC. https://www.ipcc.ch/sr15/

Goodall, J. (n.d.). *Quote by JANE GOODALL.* Deepstash. https://deepstash.com/
idea/250187/here-we-are-arguably-the-most-intelligent-being-thats-ever

Gray Wolves increase tourism in Yellowstone National Park. (2011, June 21). Yellowstone National Park. https://www.yellowstonepark.com/news/gray-
wolves-increase-tourism-in-yellowstone-national-park

Hamilton, H., Smyth, R. L., Young, B. E., Howard, T. G., Tracey, C., Breyer, S.,
Cameron, D. R., Chazal, A., Conley, A. K., Frye, C., & Schloss, C. (2022).
Increasing taxonomic diversity and spatial resolution clarifies opportunities
for protecting US imperiled species. *Ecological Application, 32*(3). https://doi.
org/10.1002/eap.2534

Hance, J., & Kessler, R. (2016, May 3). *How big donors and corporations shape
conservation goals.* Mongabay. https://news.mongabay.com/2016/05/big-
donors-corporations-shape-conservation-goals/

Heisman, R. (2018, May 24). *Bald Eagles Are the Endangered Species Act's Greatest
Success Story.* American Bird Conservancy. https://abcbirds.org/bald-eagle-
the-ultimate-endangered-species-act-success-story/

How does climate change affect biodiversity? (n.d.). Royal Society. https://royalsoci
ety.org/topics-policy/projects/biodiversity/climate-change-and-biodiver
sity/

How to Increase Biodiversity in Green Spaces Near You. (n.d.). Project Learning
Tree. https://www.plt.org/educator-tips/how-increase-biodiversity

How to start a career in wildlife conservation. (2023, January 20). GVI. https://
www.gvi.co.uk/blog/smb-how-to-start-a-career-in-wildlife-conservation/

The impact of climate change on our planet's animals. (2022, February 28).
International Fund for Animal Welfare. https://www.ifaw.org/uk/journal/
impact-climate-change-animals

Impacts of air pollution on ecosystems. (2022, November 24). European Environment Agency. https://www.eea.europa.eu/publications/air-quality-in-europe-2022/impacts-of-air-pollution-on-ecosystems

Invasive Alien Species: what they are and how they affect - Iberdrola. (n.d.). Iberdrola. https://www.iberdrola.com/sustainability/invasive-species

Irwin, S. (n.d.). *Quote by Steve Irwin: "If we can teach people about wildlife, they will..."* Goodreads. https://www.goodreads.com/quotes/6087-if-we-can-teach-people-about-wildlife-they-will-be

Joosse, T. (2021, September 7). *Wolf Populations Drop as More States Allow Hunting.* Scientific American. https://www.scientificamerican.com/article/wolf-populations-drop-as-more-states-allow-hunting/

Karaiva, P., & Marvier, M. (2012, November). What Is Conservation Science? *BioScience, 62*(11), 962-969. https://doi.org/10.1525/bio.2012.62.11.5

Knight, J. (n.d.). *THE BASICS OF WILDLIFE MANAGEMENT.* Animal Range. https://animalrange.montana.edu/documents/extension/thebasic sofwildlifemgmt.pdf

Levin, S. A. (Ed.). (2013). *Encyclopedia of Biodiversity* (Second Edition ed.). Elsevier Science. https://www.sciencedirect.com/topics/earth-and-planetary-sciences/wildlife-management

Lewis, O. (2023, July 7). *How do we measure Biodiversity and species richness?* Joe's Blooms. https://www.joesblooms.com/how-do-we-measure-biodiversity-and-species-richness

Low genetic variation. (n.d.). Understanding Evolution. https://evolution.berke ley.edu/the-relevance-of-evolution/conservation/low-genetic-variation/

Maitland, A., Lawson, M., Stroot, H., Poidatz, A., Khalfan, A., & Dabi, N. (2022, November). *Carbon billionaires: The investment emissions of the world's richest people.* Oxfam Digital Repository. https://webassets.oxfamamerica.org/media/documents/bn-carbon-billlionaires-071122-en.pdf

Maizland, L. (2023, September 15). *Global Climate Agreements: Successes and Failures.* Council on Foreign Relations. Retrieved November 6, 2023, from https://www.cfr.org/backgrounder/paris-global-climate-change-agree ments

Manning, A. (2021, November 17). *Genetic diversity gives wild populations their best chance at long-term survival.* Phys.org. https://phys.org/news/2021-11-genetic-diversity-wild-populations-chance.html

Mapes, L. V. (2023, September 10). *How the humpback whale made a massive come-back in the Salish Sea.* The Seattle Times. https://www.seattletimes.com/seat

tle-news/environment/how-the-humpback-whale-made-a-massive-comeback-in-the-salish-sea/

Mark Carwardine's advice about getting a career in conservation. (n.d.). Mark Carwardine. https://www.markcarwardine.com/wildlife-conservation/careers-in-conservation.html

Morrel, V. (2022, January 31). *Massive wolf kill disrupts long-running study of Yellowstone park packs.* Science. https://www.science.org/content/article/massive-wolf-kill-disrupts-long-running-study-yellowstone-park-packs

National Geographic Society. (2023, October 19). *Wildlife Conservation.* National Geographic Education. https://education.nationalgeographic.org/resource/wildlife-conservation/

New report shows just 100 companies are source of over 70% of emissions. (2017, July 10). CDP. https://www.cdp.net/en/articles/media/new-report-shows-just-100-companies-are-source-of-over-70-of-emissions

Our global food system is the primary driver of biodiversity loss. (2021, February 3). UNEP. https://www.unep.org/news-and-stories/press-release/our-global-food-system-primary-driver-biodiversity-loss

Pavid, K. (n.d.). *What is biodiversity and why does its loss matter?* Natural History Museum. https://www.nhm.ac.uk/discover/what-is-biodiversity.html

Plumer, B., & Popovich, N. (2021, November 12). *Who Has The Most Historical Responsibility for Climate Change?* The New York Times. https://www.nytimes.com/interactive/2021/11/12/climate/cop26-emissions-compensation.html

Predator Control as a Tool in Wildlife Management. (n.d.). Texas A&M AgriLife. https://agrilife.org/txwildlifeservices/files/2011/07/PredatorControlfor WildlifeMgt.pdf

The Pros and Cons of Working in Wildlife Conservation. (2012, February 1). Gap Africa Projects. https://gapafricaprojects.com/blog/2012/02/01/the-pros-and-cons-of-working-in-wildlife-conservation/

Ruiz, S. (2020, April 29). *How Scientists Measure Biodiversity Global Forest Watch Content.* Global Forest Watch. https://www.globalforestwatch.org/blog/data-and-research/how-scientists-measure-biodiversity/

S, A. (2023, January 30). *Classification of Animals: The Complete Guide.* AZ Animals. https://a-z-animals.com/reference/animal-classification/

Sheridan, K. (n.d.). *Culling: A Controversial Tool In Wildlife Conservation – Kate Sheridan.* SheSapiens. https://shesapiens.com/culling-in-wildlife-conservation/

6 Ways to Preserve Biodiversity | Yale Sustainability. (2020, October 1). Yale Sustainability. https://sustainability.yale.edu/blog/6-ways-preserve-biodiversity

Stop Wildlife Crime. (n.d.). WWF. https://www.worldwildlife.org/pages/stop-wildlife-crime

Strategy for halting and reversing biodiversity loss revealed. (2020, September). UNEP-WCMC. https://www.unep-wcmc.org/en/news/strategy-for-halting-and-reversing-biodiversity-loss-revealed

Taxonomic Classification of Animals with Examples. (2022, November 27). Earth Reminder. https://www.earthreminder.com/taxonomic-classification-of-animals/

10 Important Pros and Cons of Culling Animals. (2023, September 26). Our Endangered World. https://www.ourendangeredworld.com/pros-and-cons-of-culling-animals/

Thekaekara, T. (2018, June 27). *Can we live harmoniously with wildlife? - Open-Learn - Open University.* The Open University. https://www.open.edu/openlearn/nature-environment/environmental-studies/can-we-live-harmoniously-wildlife

Three Levels of Biodiversity. (n.d.). Canadian Biodiversity. https://canadianbiodiversity.mcgill.ca/english/theory/threelevels.htm

Tolme, P. (2017, January 30). *The U.S. Biodiversity Crisis.* National Wildlife Federation. https://www.nwf.org/Magazines/National-Wildlife/2017/Feb-March/Conservation/Biodiversity

Ultimate Guide to Wildlife Conservation Jobs. (2023, May 17). Ecology Project International. https://www.ecologyproject.org/post/how-to-get-your-dream-job-working-in-animal-conservation

van Aarde, R. J., & Jackson, T. P. (2007). Megaparks for metapopulations: Addressing the causes of locally high elephant numbers in southern Africa. *Biological Conservation, 134*(3), 289-297. https://doi.org/10.1016/j.biocon.2006.08.027

van Wyk, K. (2016, June 9). *Alternatives to Culling As a Means of Wildlife Population Control.* The Serial Comma. https://rooseveltwritersnl.blogspot.com/2016/06/alternatives-to-culling-as-means-of.html

Watson, S. K. (2022, March 14). *Map shows at-risk species are in Americans' backyards.* Popular Science. https://www.popsci.com/environment/map-endangered-species-us/

Waugh, C. (2022, July 7). *Corporations vs. Consumers: Who is really to blame for climate change?* the University of Manchester WordPress Websites & Blogs. https://sites.manchester.ac.uk/global-social-challenges/2022/07/07/corpo rations-vs-consumers-who-is-really-to-blame-for-climate-change/

What are the pros and cons of "rewilding" ? Using examples of Britain and the USA. (2016, November 10). Min Muses. https://minsblogweb.wordpress.com/ 2016/11/10/what-are-the-pros-and-cons-of-rewilding-using-examples-of-britain-and-the-usa/

What is Biodiversity? Why Is It Important? (n.d.). American Museum of Natural History. https://www.amnh.org/research/center-for-biodiversity-conserva tion/what-is-biodiversity

What is the goal of wildlife conservation? (2022, March 4). FutureLearn. https:// www.futurelearn.com/info/blog/goal-of-wildlife-conserva tion#What_is_the_goal_of_wildlife_conservation

Who is responsible for climate change? (2022, November 7). Oxfam. https://www. oxfamamerica.org/explore/stories/who-is-responsible-for-climate-change/

Wildlife Management Practices. (n.d.). Bowhunter Ed. https://www.bowhunter-ed.com/national/studyGuide/Wildlife-Management-Practices/ 301099_185360/

Yarrow, G. (n.d.). *Wildlife and Wildlife Management.* South Carolina State Library Digital Collection. https://dc.statelibrary.sc.gov/bitstream/handle/10827/ 41263/CU_ES_FNR_Fact_Sheet_36_2009-05.pdf

Made in United States
Orlando, FL
26 November 2024

54501641R00125